HANGED
What if he was innocent?

Dr. Binoy Gupta

Copyright © 2008 Binoy Gupta
All rights reserved.

ISBN: 1-4196-8183-4
ISBN-13: 9781419681837

Visit www.booksurge.com to order additional copies.

"I had……………..come to an entirely erroneous conclusion which shows, my dear Watson, how dangerous it always is to reason from insufficient data."

—Sherlock Holmes
in Arthur Conan Doyle's…
The Adventure of the Speckled Band.

You can not come to correct conclusions unless you know the facts…This book will give you a wealth of information about Capital Punishment.

It will take you on a vivid journey through two centuries of experimentation with Capital Punishment.

—Binoy Gupta

Contents

1. Foreword by Hon'ble Justice Krishna Iyer — 9
2. Introduction — 15
3. Background — 19
4. Day 1 — 27
   History of Capital Punishment (U.K.) — 31
   Homicide Act 1957 — 34
   Capital Punishment Abolished — 35
   Timothy Evans — 38
   Mahmood Hussein Mattan — 41
   Bentley and Craig — 43
   James Hanratty — 48
   Birmingham Six — 51
5. Day 2 — 57
   History of Capital Punishment (U.S.) — 57
   Nicola Sacco and Bartolomeo Vanzetti — 62
   Bruno Richard Hauptmann — 63
   Scottsboro Boys — 66
   Caryl Chessman — 68
   Julius and Ethel Rosenberg — 71
6. Day 3 — 79
   History of Capital Punishment (U.S.) continued — 79
   Ronald Cotton — 79
   Kirk Bloodworth — 82
   Ray Krone — 85
   Orenthal James Simpson — 87

7.	Day 4	97
	History of Capital Punishment (Canada)	97
	David Milgaard	101
	Donald Marshall	103
	Thomas Sophonow	105
	Guy Paul Morin	107
	Robert Baltovich	109
8.	Day 5	115
	History of Capital Punishment (Australia)	115
	Lindy Chamberlain Creighton	116
	Ronald Ryan	118
9.	Day 6	127
	Amnesty International	127
	Kenny Richey	134
10.	Day 7	139
	United Nations and Capital Punishment	139
	Universal Declaration of Human Rights	139
	International Covenant on Civil and Political Rights	142
	Second Optional Protocol	142
	Convention on the Rights of the Child	143
11.	Day 8	151
	Europe and Capital Punishment	151
	Council of Europe and Capital Punishment	151
	Protocol Nos. 6, 11 and 13	153
	European Union and Capital Punishment	
	First World Congress against the Death Penalty	160
	Second World Congress against the Death Penalty	163
	Third World Congress against the Death Penalty	163

12.	Day 9	173
	India and Capital Punishment	173
	Bachan Singh vs. State of Punjab	173
	Smt. Triveniben vs. State of Gujarat	174
	Dhananjoy Chatterjee vs. State of W. B.	174
	State of Uttar Pradesh vs. Devendra Singh	179
	Rajendra Prasad's case and two other cases	181
	Lalla Singh's case	190
13.	Day 10	195
	Final Submissions	196
	DNA Testing	196
	T. N. Vatheeswaran vs State of Tamil Nadu	199
	Sher Singh and others vs State of Punjab	200
	Smt. Triveniben vs. State of Gujarat	200
	The End - Ravi Samant is Hanged and found innocent	207
	My Last Thoughts and dedication of this book	211

V. R. Krishna Iyer
Fax and Phone: 0484 2370088
(Former Judge, Supreme Court) "SATYAGAMAYA"
M.G.ROAD, ERNAKULUM
KOCHI - 682011
Email: satgamya@dataone.in
Website:www.vrkrishnaiyer.org

FOREWORD

I am an abolitionist because my compassionate heart beats to the nuances of Mahatma Gandhi's and his Ahimsa. He has said that God has given life and God alone can take it. Therefore, life-depriving processes of homicide by hanging or otherwise under judicial command cannot be justified to violation to the sacred preservation of life. Death sentence runs the risk of innocent persons being executed. In my judgment in the Supreme Court, I was against death sentence and Lord Scarman, sitting in the Privy Coucil, appreciated my judgments on the subject, followed them in his judgment (though in a minority). In 1977, the Amnesty International held an International Conference against death penalty and invited me, then a judge of the Supreme Court of India, to inaugurate it along with Prime Minister Olaf Palme, Sweden's Prime Minister. The venue was Stockholm.

I wholly agree with the theme of the author of the book "Hanged, What if he was innocent" that Capital punishment should be abolished as guiltless people may suffer execution by judicial error. The narration by the author of an innocent youth being hanged and his innocence discovered a day later in vain is not uncommon. What a terrible crime? I take the liberty of reproducing an actual instance from a book by Justice A.S.P. Ayyar "25 Years a Civilian":

The Sub-Collector's bungalow was a big and spacious one, but had no compound walls and was situated in the same compound as the District Judge's Bungalow and the District Medical Officer's Bungalow. One room in the even bigger District Judge's Bungalow was not used, the reason assigned being that a previous District Judge had committed suicide there. He had sentenced a man to death for murder, though the man had protested that he was at Chicacole, miles away from the scene of murder, at the time he was alleged to have committed the murder, and thus could never have committed the murder. The sentence was confirmed by the High Court and the man duly hanged. Some time after that, the man's spirit is said to have appeared before the District Judge in his sleep at 2 a.m. at night and told him, "It is you who have committed the murder and not I. If you go and look up the records in the Chicacole Sub-Collector' office, you would find that in a mahazar I have been noted as having been present there that day. The conscientious District Judge, an Englishman, took his car and went to Chicacole and found that the statement was true. The man had not been able to mention it when alive as he did not know that his presence was noted in the mahazar. The District Judge is then said to have taken his own life on the principle enunciate in Hammarabi's law, "A life for a life". His example is reminiscent of the Ancient Tamil King Neduncheziyan who died of shock on realising that he had wrongly sentenced Kovalan to death for a crime he did not commit.

In presenting the important topic of abolition of the capital punishment through an imaginative case where the victim hanged was subsequently found to be innocent, the author has tried to bring together into one coherent view the background history of capital punishment in the major countries of the world; the views of Amnesty International, International covenant on civil rights and the importance of DNA testing.

The author has succeeded in pointing out the obscurities in the principle of coming to a conclusion on circumstantial evidence alone and has noted the apparent incongruencies between many of the implications and our moral sentiments.

More than half the world, including UK and commonwealth countries, have abolished death sentence. So has Phillipines. The United Nations itself have, by resolution, abolished death penalty. Those countries which have not may well be classified as barbaric. It is my conviction that India in its penological reform from Macaulay to Mahatma will wipe out the bloodstained sentence of judicial verdict. I wish the author's vision universal acceptance.

July 20, 2006   V. R. KRISHNA IYER

Whoever commits murder shall be punished with death, or imprisonment for life, and shall also be liable to fine.

Old Section 302 of the Indian Penal Code

Concepts of social justice have varied with age and clime. If it could be possible for Confusius, Manu, Hammurabi and Solomon to meet together at a conference table, I doubt whether they would be able to evolve agreed formulae as to what constitutes social justice, which is a very controversial field.... In countries with democratic forms of Government public opinion and the law act and react on each other.

Balakrishna Iyer, J.

Introduction

All my life, I have been a student of law. I acquired three degrees in law. Bachelors degree from Calcutta University. Masters degree from Madras University. And Ph.D., the highest academic degree, from Bombay University. Besides, I acquired a number of post graduate diplomas in various subjects - including Cyber Laws.

I have watched the Indian judicial system closely. I have been a victim as well as beneficiary of the Indian judicial system. It is expensive. It is time consuming. And like any other system, sometimes it blunders. After all, judges, too, are human. But the consequences of an erroneous judgement can be disastrous.

Just to give a real life example. I filed a case in the Central Administrative Tribunal in 1980. The Tribunal is expected to dispose off cases expeditiously. In September 2005, after 25 years, even as I stood on the verge of retirement from government service, the case was far from over. In 2004, the Central Administrative Tribunal accepted that the order passed by it in 1989 was wrong. Yet, within six months of its earlier decision, the same judges again held that the order passed in 1989 was right! And though I was very much in service, in their order, they have surprisingly observed that I had retired from service. I do know from where the Hon'ble judges got this wrong notion! But the system is such, that even to get such an apparent mistake corrected is extremely difficult. Once again, the chain of litigation has to be set in motion.

This book is a pure novel. Perhaps my character is based on Dhananjoy Chatterjee. But the similarity ends there. I have never met him. Perhaps you, too, have never seen him. This novel covers the serious issue of capital punishment; and will gently guide you through the complex issue and will finally lead you to the vexing question whether capital punishment is right or wrong.

The issue is complex. The issue transcedents all geographical barriers and concerns all nations. The issue is universal. And there is no simple answer.
A poor, ill-educated, person like Dhananjoy Chatterjee, would hardly understand the legal procedures and complexities. He and his family members would not have enough money even to engage a mediocre lawyer.

Dhananjoy Chatterjee was hanged to death. Whether he committed the rape and murder, I do not know. Whether hanging him was right or wrong, I do not know. The only question which lingers in my thoughts, and constantly plagues me in my dreams, is *What if he was innocent* ?

I have tried to depict what happens in the convict's family after a death sentence is passed. I have tried to show how judges, politicians, governors and presidents act. I have presented a number of real cases where innocent persons have been sentenced to death. Some have been executed. Others have been lucky and just escaped death. In some cases, the concerned governments have admitted their mistake and even given substantial monetary compensation.

I have presented the reactions of and the arguments advanced by the pro and anti capital punishment lobbies. I have given the stands taken by several international organizations - UNO, European Union, Amnesty International, etc. Underlying the entire sequence of events is the hype created by the media which certainly influences public thinking.

Please go through this book patiently, impassionately. Keep your mind and heart open. After that, make your own decision. Arrive at your own conclusion whether capital punishment is right or wrong. Decide whether capital punishment should be retained or not.

Binoy Gupta

The Back Ground

Ruby Mehta, a 16 year old girl, lived with her parents in a third floor flat of one of the buildings in Central Bombay. Ravi Savant was a watchman in the same building.

Every morning, Ruby would go to school. Ravi Savant, the watchman would usually be on duty. His duty hours were 12 hours - from 8 A.M. to 8 P.M. - practically all the seven days of the week. He liked Ruby. Sometimes, he would offer her a sweet or toffee. Sometimes, he would talk with her about her school, about her teachers, about her friends.

One day, Ruby went to school but did not return. After a couple of days, her body was found. Medical examination confirmed that she had been raped on March 5, 1990. After the rape, she had been strangulated to death.

The police started investigations immediately. Ravi Savant was found missing. He was arrested in his village - a small one near Pune (about 200 kilometres from Bombay). He was charged with the offences of committing the rape and murder.

No one had seen Ravi Savant commit the rape or murder. Based entirely on circumstantial evidence, a Bombay magistrate found Ravi Savant guilty of committing the rape and murder of the 16 year old girl and sentenced him to life imprisonment.

The Maharashtra Government filed an appeal before the High Court of Bombay for enhancement of the sentence of life imprisonment to that of death. In January 1994, after a brief hearing, the Bombay High Court enhanced the sentence of life imprisonment to that of death.

Ravi Savant preferred appeal before the Supreme Court of India. In June 1994, the Supreme Court upheld the verdict of the Bombay High Court and confirmed the death sentence.

Two options were now open to Ravi Savant. He could file a clemency petition before the Governor of Maharashtra or before the President of India. He submitted a mercy petition before the Governor of Maharashtra.

In July 1994, Ravi Savant obtained a stay on his execution from the Bombay High Court, pending consideration of the mercy petitions first by the Governor of Maharashtra; and then by the President of the India - should such an application be filed.

The Governor of Maharashtra dismissed the mercy petition in September 1994. Ravi Savant submitted a mercy petition to the President of India. In December 1994, the President rejected the mercy petition.

The stay of execution granted by the Bombay High Court continued till 2007 for the simple reason that no one told the Court that the mercy petitions had been dismissed by the Governor of Maharashtra and also by the President of India.

In December 2007, the Maharashtra Government requested the Bombay High Court to vacate the stay of execution on the ground that Ravi Savant's mercy petitions had been rejected more than a decade ago. The Bombay High Court vacated the stay the same month.

Ravi Savant then filed a writ petition seeking a stay of his execution and commutation of the death sentence. A Division Bench of the Bombay High Court dismissed this petition in December 2007. He also sent a petition to the Governor of Maharashtra requesting commutation of his death sentence. The Governor dismissed his petition in January 2008.

Ravi Savant challenged the Governor's order in the Bombay High Court on the ground of non-application of mind as to the mitigating circumstances of his case. He submitted that the Governor was not apprised of the material facts of the case and had gone solely by the nature of the crime committed. He claimed that the Governor had dismissed the mercy petition without following the established procedure. The Bombay High Court directed the Governor to apply his mind and re-examine the application. Once again, the Governor rejected the petition.

Ravi Savant submitted a mercy petition to the President of India. The President sought the Union Home Ministry's opinion on his mercy petition. In the meantime, the President's office asked the Maharashtra Government to stay his execution till the President had decided on the application.

Acting on the advice of the Union Home Ministry, and after consultations with the Attorney-General of India, in February 2008, the President rejected the mercy petition.

By this time, Ravi Savant's case was gaining momentum. Open any newspaper, any magazine, Ravi Savant would be on the first page. The issue of capital punishment became the hottest topic of the day. Both pro and anti capital punishment lobbies were holding meetings and organizing rallies. There were numerous articles both for and against capital punishment.

Time was running out for Ravi Savant. The Governor of Maharashtra, the President of India, and the Bombay High Court had all given a go ahead to his execution. Now only the Supreme Court of India could do anything.

Some friends and well wishers of Ravi Savant decided to approach the Supreme Court of India for commutation of the death sentence. Good lawyers are very expensive. They did not have the money. Finally, they approached a group of young lawyers and requested them to file the application before the Supreme Court of India.

The young lawyers agreed to fight the case in the Supreme Court. They knew this was one of the worst cases. They knew they had a lost case. But they were determined to make every effort possible to get a reprieve.

All over the country, groups of girls, ladies and others were baying for Ravi Savant's blood. A young girl had been raped and brutally murdered. The murderer deserved the death sentence…… nothing less!

A group of ladies had even managed to rope in the wife of the Chief Minister of Maharashtra. She led processions and held public rallies demanding the execution of Ravi Savant.

Anti capital punishment organizations, like the Amnesty International and smaller organizations, held their own meetings and rallies. They sent letters, petitions and emails to every one including the United Nations and Human Rights Commissions pleading that having regard to the facts and circumstances, the death sentence should be reduced to one of life.

The young lawyers realized that the hype the media had created was working against Ravi Savant. They worked very hard. They went through all the decisions on capital punishment. They collected material from other countries. And they decided to work out an effective and meaningful strategy.

They selected a Punjabi girl, Pretty Singh, the most brilliant lawyer of the group, to argue the case. Pretty was tall. She was very beautiful. She had glamour. She had poise. She was intelligent. And she had a soft, scintillating, silver voice. If any one could make the judges listen, it was Pretty.

The Supreme Court had ruled that a sentence of death should be commuted to one of life imprisonment if there had been undue delay in execution. Pretty decided to make this legal proposition the foundation of her arguments.

Pretty decided to start from the basics. She would start with the history of capital punishment in U.K. How it had been gradually abolished in that country. The experience of other countries, like the U.S., Canada and Australia. She would highlight a few cases where innocent persons had been executed or just escaped the gallows. She would submit to the court all the reasons for and against capital punishment.

The question was whether the hard-pressed-for-time Supreme Court judges would allow Pretty to say all this. She decided to request the judges to give her an hour's hearing every day for 2 weeks - 10 working days in all. If the judges agreed, she would be able to tell the Court all that she wanted to tell. She knew the media would publish all this. This could soften public sentiment and hopefully tilt the final decision in Ravi Savant's favour.

Meanwhile, Ravi Savant's father, mother, wife and two children sat in their small hut in a little village in Maharashtra. They were desperate and shattered. They were certain of his innocence. In any event, he had suffered enough - 18 years in jail. That alone was more than enough!

Ravi Savant's wife was inconsolate. At times, she felt desperate. Sometimes, she would see a flicker of hope. She knew that time was running out - fast. But without any reason, she hoped a miracle would occur and her husband would escape the gallows.

The family had spent all they had on lawyers and courts. They had sold their land long ago. The little pieces of jewellery the wife and mother had had also been sold long ago. Ever so often, there was not enough food for the family.Sometimes, the elders had to manage without any meal. If only they had money, they could have hired good lawyers. Probably, things would have been different.

Many of the Judges of England have said that they do not make law. They only interpret it.

This is an illusion which they have fostered. But it is a notion which is now being discarded everywhere.

Every new decision - on every new situation - is a development of the law.

Lord Dennings

Day 1

This is Supreme Court of India's Court Room No. 1. The trial of Ravi Savant is to begin at 10.30 A.M. The Court Room is packed. The front chairs are occupied by black robed lawyers. The back benches by journalists, friends, some persons in favour of the capital punishment and others against it. A large number of persons are waiting outside the court room.

The Chief Justice had declined to hear the case because in a recent conference, he had strongly argued for retention of the capital punishment. He had selected a lady judge, but she felt she would not be able to bear the strain. She, too, had refused to hear the case. Finally, two senior judges had been selected to hear the much publicized case.

The Maharashtra Government had requested the Solicitor General of India to argue the case. The Solicitor General and his team of lawyers are confident of the outcome.

Pretty Singh, the young lawyer looks a little nervous. This is her first case before the apex court. She is intelligent. She is brilliant. She is a superb speaker. But this is a difficult case. She has spent almost an entire month on this case. She looks around, folds her hands towards the sky and sits down. Perhaps she has silently mumbled a prayer.

There is pin drop silence. Someone's wrist watch alarm suddenly shatters the silence. It is 10.30 A.M. The mace-bearers of the judges announce their arrival. The two judges enter the Court Room, bow and sit down.

Justice A: You may begin.
Pretty: My Lordships. This case concerns the life and liberty of a poor, innocent victim. I…….

Justice B: Why do you call your client innocent? He has committed rape and murder. He has already been convicted and sentenced to death.

Pretty: My Lordships. I have the right to call my client innocent. I request your Lordships to treat him as innocent until your Lordships arrive at a different conclusion. And that your Lordships should do only after your Lordships have heard the arguments, examined the evidence and arrived at a considered conclusion.

If your Lordships treat him as a rapist and a murderer right from the beginning, then all I can say is he has lost the case even before the trial has begun. And I will take the liberty of saying that your Lordships have pre judged him even before the trial has begun.

Justice A: No…No. We have not pre judged your client. Our minds are open. We would like to give your client a fair trial. But the legal position is very clear. His trial is already over. He has been found guilty and sentenced to death. We will only hear whether he is entitled to commutation of his death sentence.

Pretty: My Lordships. This is my first case before the highest court of the country. The issue concerns a human life. If I transgress a little, or if I commit any errors, I crave your pardon.

Justice A: Please carry on.

Pretty: This case has already received too much publicity in the media and the decision in this case will have a bearing on a large number of cases pending in various courts throughout the country. The decision will also have a bearing on the fate of a large number of convicts awaiting execution. I humbly request that the hearing be spread over 10 days - one hour every day for 10 mornings - spread over two weeks. This way, the court's day to day work will not suffer.

Solicitor General: What a preposterous request. We have other cases.

Justice A and Justice B talk to each other.

Justice A: We have promised you a fair trial. Your request is granted. The case will be heard over the next two weeks beginning today - one hour every working day. But no further....Please keep this in mind. Mr. Solicitor General. We are dealing with some one's life. We have a young upcoming lawyer. We are sure we can fulfill this little wish. We seek your indulgence.

Solicitor General: As your Lordships wish.

Pretty: My Lordships. I am greatly honoured. I will now begin my submissions. I propose to put forth three arguments.

- Argument No. 1: My client is innocent. There is no evidence to prove that he committed either the rape or the subsequent murder.
- Argument No. 2: Presuming he is guilty, is this case one of those rare of the rarest cases, where a death sentence is called for?
- Argument No. 3: Presuming again that he is guilty, and even presuming that this indeed is one those rare of the rarest cases, where a death sentence is called for, does not the long delay of more than 18 years in executing him, the pain and suffering he has undergone, entitle him to commutation of the death sentence at this stage?

Justice B: The convict has already been found guilty and sentenced to death. We will hear you only on the question whether the death sentence should be commuted to imprisonment for life or not.

Pretty: My Lordships. I am only asking your Lordships to commute the death sentence. But all that I am going to submit before your Lordships over the next ten days will have a bearing on this.

If there is no evidence to show that Ravi Savant is guilty; if I can show that this is not one of the rarest of rare cases where the death penalty has to be imposed; or even if I am able to convince your Lordships that there has been undue delay in execution of the death sentence, he is entitled to commutation of his death sentence.

History of Capital Punishment (U.K.)

Pretty: My Lordships. The Indian legal system and Indian criminal laws are based on the British criminal law. I will take your Lordships through the history of capital punishment in Britain and its eventual abolishment.

Solicitor General: Madam. We all know the history of capital punishment. You are wasting the Honourable Court's time and also our time.

Pretty: Respected Solicitor General sir. Kindly bear with me. I promise I will not take more than the 10 hours I have asked for and have been granted.

Justice A: You may continue.

Pretty: My Lordships. Britain had capital punishment for more than 200 offences - including some extremely trivial offences. In 1808, Sir Samuel Romilly introduced reforms to abolish the death penalty for some of the capital offences in what he termed England's "Bloody Code". Examples of some such offences are:

- Being in the company of gypsies for one month;
- Vagrancy for soldiers and sailors; and
- Strong evidence of malice in children aged 7-14 years of age.

Between 1832 and 1834, British Parliament abolished the death penalty for:

- Shoplifting of goods worth five shillings or less;
- Returning from transportation;

- Letter-stealing; and
- Sacrilege.

The removal of capital punishment for crimes which was out of all proportion to the crime committed, actually increased the number of convictions. The reason was that when convictions for these offences carried the capital punishment, instead of awarding the capital punishment, the judges acquitted the convicts. After removal of the death sentence for these offences, judges passed sentences which they viewed more appropriate.

Barbarian and obnoxious though this practice may appear today, Britain had the practice of Gibbeting - the public display of executed corpses in cages. This was abolished in 1843.

In 1861, the number of crimes which carried the capital punishment was reduced to four:

- Murder;
- Treason;
- Arson in royal dockyards; and
- Piracy with violence.

Public execution was stopped in 1868. The hanging, beheading and quartering of traitors was stopped in 1870.

At the beginning of the century, the mandatory punishment for murder was death by hanging. No other sentence was allowed in law. The convict was permitted only one appeal to the Court of Criminal Appeal on the grounds of conviction. For example, on the ground of the judge misdirecting the jury and incorrect points of law. That was the only appeal allowed to the courts.

Only if the Attorney General considered that any case contained important points of law, he could refer the case to the House of Lords (the highest court in Britain).

A jury could make a "recommendation to mercy" to the Home Secretary, but he could disregard this. The Home Secretary had the power to commute the death sentence to one of life imprisonment. But if he decided not to interfere and allowed the law to take its course, that was the end of the matter. In addition, the Home Secretary could ask for a medical panel to assess the condemned prisoner's mental condition.

In 1938, the House of Commons voted for legislation to abolish capital punishment in peace time on an experimental basis for a period of five-years. Then World War II broke out. There was no progress. Two later attempts to pass similar legislation were blocked by the House of Lords and then side-stepped by Labour and Conservative governments.

After the end of the war in 1945, partly due to the extensive coverage given by the media; partly because of several notable cases which indicated that several innocent persons had been wrongly convicted and even executed; the diverse and opposite views of the pro and anti capital punishment organizations, in 1948, the Labour government appointed a Royal Commission on the Death Penalty. As a follow up of the Royal Commission's report, the Conservative government came up with a compromise legislation - the Homicide Act of 1957.

Homicide Act 1957

Pretty: The Homicide Act 1957 restricted capital punishment in murder cases to five types of murder:

- Murder in the course or furtherance of theft; Murder by shooting or causing an explosion;
- Murder while resisting arrest or during an escape;
- Murder of a police officer or prison officer; and
- Two murders committed on different occasions.

These classifications themselves introduced some arbitrariness and unfairness. Why should someone who strangles a person not be hanged, when someone who shoots another should be executed? Murder in the course of theft was punishable by death, but murder in the course of rape was not. This fuelled further public disquiet against the death penalty. Judges do not like to award the capital punishment. Capital murder convictions became less common.

Even after the passing of the Homicide Act 1957, there were still several instances where miscarriages of justice have been suspected. For example, the case of James Hanratty who was executed on April 4, 1962, at Bedford Prison, for the shooting of Michael Gregsten.

The last executions in Britain were of two men on August 13, 1964. Peter Anthony Allen (aged 21) was hanged in Walton jail, Liverpool and Gwynne Owen Evans (aged 24) was hanged in Strangeways, Manchester. They were both convicted of the murder of John Alan West, while robbing him in his house on April 7, 1964.

Capital Punishment Abolished

Pretty: In 1965, the British Parliament passed Sidney Silverman's Private Member's Bill which suspended the death penalty for murder for five years. This was the fourth time that the House of Commons had voted for abolition, but the first time it actually became law.

Just before the Bill, which is known as the Murder (Abolition of the Death Penalty) Act 1965, received the Royal Assent, the Home Office allowed the reburial of Timothy Evans outside Pentonville prison. It was the start of a process which led to Timothy Evans being granted a posthumous free pardon in October 1966.

In 1969, Parliament finally abolished the death penalty - even for murder. In 1973, Parliament abolished the death penalty permanently, even in Northern Ireland.

After the abolition of capital punishment, there have been several famous cases of miscarriages of justice which would have resulted in executions, if that option had been available. A good example of this is the Birmingham Six case.

Since 1969, there have been over a dozen attempts to reintroduce capital punishment for various categories of murder. All have failed. The trend has been towards more and more MPs voting in Parliament in favour of abolition.

In fact since 1945, three convicts have received posthumous pardons:

- Timothy Evans in 1966;
- Mahood Mattan in 1998; and
- Derek Bentley also in 1998.

After abolition of the capital punishment for murder, the death sentence had remained in force for treason and piracy with violence. Under the Crime and Disorder Act, use of capital punishment in these two instances also was abolished in 1998.

On January 27, 1999, the U.K. Home Secretary (Labour MP Jack Straw) signed the 6th protocol of the European Convention of Human Rights in Strasbourg. This move has formally abolished the death penalty in U.K.

Notable Dates

Pretty: My Lordships. I will submit a list of some important dates in the history of capital punishment:

1908	People under 16 can not be hanged.
1922	Infanticide (Mother killing her child) no longer a capital offence.

1931	Pregnant women can not be hanged.
1933	People under 18 can not be hanged. They can be sentenced to imprisonment till Her/His Majesty's pleasure.
1948	House of Commons suspends capital punishment. Over ruled by House of Lords.
March 9, 1950	Timothy John Evans hanged at Pentonville Prison.
January 28, 1953	Derek Bentley hanged at Wandsworth Prison for the murder of P.C. Miles.
July 13, 1955	Ruth Ellis, the last Women to be hanged in U.K., is hanged at Holloway Prison.
1956	The passing of Death Penalty (Abolition) Bill is overturned by House of Lords.
1957	Homicide Act 1957 restricts use of capital punishment.
July 23, 1957	John Vickers is executed - the first execution under the 1957 Act.
November 5, 1959	Gunther Podola is executed-the last execution for murder of a police officer.
August 13, 1964	Peter Anthony Allen & Gwynne Owen Evans are executed - the last executions in U.K.
1965	Capital punishment in murder cases is suspended for 5 years.
1966	Timothy John Evans receives posthumous pardon.
1969	Capital punishment for murder is abolished.

February 1998	Mahmood Mattan receives posthumous pardon.
July 1998	Derek Bentley receives posthumous pardon.
March 1999	James Hanratty case is referred back to the Court of Criminal Appeal.
May 2002	The Court of Criminal Appeal confirms James Hanratty's sentence.

Pretty: My Lordships. I will show that even in a country like U.K., which prides itself with the finest judicial system in the world, there have been several cases of miscarriage of justice. Several innocent persons have been sentenced to death. A few have been fortunate and escaped......but after decades of imprisonment. I will briefly take you through a few important cases.

Timothy Evans

Pretty: My Lordships. I will now take you through the case of Timothy Evans. Evans was executed on March 9, 1950 at Pentonville Prison. He was granted posthumous pardon in 1966.

In 1949, Timothy Evans (aged 24), a semi-literate van driver, his wife and infant daughter lived on the top floor of 10, Rillington Place, a grimy house in Notting Hill Gate, London. On November 30, 1949, Evans walked into a police station in Wales and reported that he had found his wife dead in their London home, and had put her body down a drain.

Later, the strangled bodies of Evans' wife and child were found in the backyard. Evans confessed to the killings. But later on, he accused John Reginald Halliday Christie (aged 54), who lived on the ground floor of the same house.

Christie who had served in the Army during World War One and been a Special Police Constable during the Second World War denied any responsibility. Evans was sentenced to death for the murder of his child, and hanged on March 9, 1950 at Pentonville Prison.

On March 24, 1953, a West Indian tenant of 10, Rillington Place found the bodies of three women in a cupboard in Christie's former flat. A fourth body was found under the floorboards of another room. The remains of two more women were found in the garden.

Christie admitted to murdering four women, including his wife, at 10, Rillington Place. He said the other three, all in their twenties, were prostitutes. He admitted to murdering two more women in 1943 and 1944 when he was a special constable in the War Reserve Police.

Christie related how he had invited women to his house, made them partly drunk, sat them in a deck-chair, where he made them unconscious with domestic coal gas. He then strangled and raped them. Among his various revelations was his admission that he had also killed Mrs. Evans, although he denied having killed the baby.

Christie's trial for his wife's murder began at the Old Bailey on June 22, 1953. His defence plea was based on insanity. The trial ended in three days. Christie was found guilty of his wife's murder; sentenced to death and hanged on July 15, 1953 at Pentonville Prison on the same gallows where Evans had been - three years earlier.

Christie had served sentences for theft and he was known as a habitual liar. In his teens, he was known as "Reggie no dick" and "Can't do it Christie" on account of his sexual inadequacy. Christie's motives in murdering the women were sexual. He was a mass murderer and sexual psychopath who had murdered at least 6 women.

The Home Secretary, Mr. David Maxwell-Fyfe, ordered a private enquiry led by a senior barrister, Mr. John Scott Henderson. The Henderson enquiry report published on July 13, 1953, two days before Christie's execution, concluded that Evans had killed both his wife and daughter.

The Henderson report became controversial. Many people felt it was a white-washing exercise intended to protect the police's inept handling of the Evans case.

On February 10, 1965, Chuter Ede (the Home Secretary at the time of Evan's execution) said that the Evans' case showed how a mistake was possible and that one had been made.

Another inquiry, headed by Mr. Justice Brabin, took place during 1965-1966. The Brabin Inquiry report found that Evans had probably killed his wife but that he had not killed his daughter. Since Evans had been convicted of his daughter Geraldine's murder, and not for the murder of his wife, Evans was granted a posthumous pardon in 1966.

Mahmood Hussein Mattan

Pretty: My Lordships. I will now take you through the case of Mahmood Hussein Mattan. Mattan was executed on September 3, 1952 at Cardiff Prison. He was granted posthumous pardon in 1998 - after 46 years.

Mattan was born in Somalia. He met his wife Laura, in the late 1940s, when he was a merchant seaman. Laura's family did not approve of the marriage due to racial differences. So they lived in a separate house in the same street in Cardiff.

On March 6, 1952, Lily Volpert (aged 42), was found murdered in her pawnbroker's shop in Cardiff's docklands area. Her throat had been slit with a razor and £ 100 had been stolen. Within hours of the discovery of her body, Mattan, (aged 28), and by now a father of three children, was arrested by the Cardiff City Police (now part of South Wales Police) and tried for the murder of Lily Volpert.

Mattan had lost his job in 1952. He liked playing cards. He was fond of gambling on greyhound races. But he had no history of any violent conduct.

The main witness at his trial at Glamorganshire Assizes in July 1952 was Harold Cover who himself was one of the initial suspects in the case. After a reward of £ 200 was offered by Lily Volpert's family (which then was sufficient to buy a house in Cardiff), Harold Cover claimed to have seen Mattan leaving Lily Volperts' premises on the night of the murder.

One of the officers investigating the Volpert case, Detective Inspector Ludon Roberts (died - 1981), was aware that Harold Cover's description did not match that of Mattan, but this point was not placed before the original trial jury. The description given by Harold Cover matched that of another Somali - Tehar Gass - who was interviewed by Cardiff City Police during their investigations. Gass admitted visiting Lily Volpert's shop on the day of the murder, but this fact was also not told to the original trial jury.

Surprisingly, Mattan's own defence barrister described him as a semi-civilized savage. The jury found Mattan guilty and the judge passed the mandatory sentence of death. In August 1952, Mattan's appeal was dismissed. On September 3, 1952, he became the last person to be hanged at Cardiff Prison. As in the case of other executed prisoners, his remains were buried within the prison.

In 1954, Gass was tried for the murder of a wages clerk called Granville Jenkins. But Gass was found insane and sent to Broadmoor. After his release, he was deported to Somalia. In 1969, Harold Cover was convicted of the attempted murder of his daughter with a razor.

After this conviction, Mattan's wife Laura approached the then Home Secretary, James Callaghan, but he did not refer the case to the Court of Appeal.

In 1996, Mahmood Mattan's remains were exhumed from Cardiff Prison and re-buried in a Cardiff Cemetery. On February 24, 1998, the Court of Appeal in London, quashed Mahmood Mattan's conviction. Lord Justice Rose (Vice-President of the Court of Appeal) said that the case against Mahmood Mattan was "demonstrably flawed". He went on to say that Mahmood Mattan's death and the length of time taken to dismiss the conviction were matters of profound regret. The other judges sitting with Lord Justice Rose were Justices Mr. Holland and Mr. Penry-Davey.

Bentley and Craig

Pretty: My Lordships. I will now take you through the unfortunate case of Derek Bentley. This is one of those cases which ultimately led to the abolition of capital punishment in Britain. On July 30, 1998, the Court of Appeal overturned the erroneous conviction and thereafter the government granted Bentley a full pardon.

On November 2, 1952, Derek Bentley (aged 19) and Christopher Craig (aged 16) broke into Barlow & Parker's Warehouse, Tanworth Road, Croydon, London. Craig had a revolver.

Some people saw them entering the premises and called the police. Bentley and Craig then went onto the flat roof of the building and hid behind a lift-housing.

Detective Sergeant Frederick Fairfax climbed on to the roof and managed to grab Bentley. Craig shouted defiantly at the detective and Bentley managed to break free.

According to the police, at this point, Bentley shouted "Let him have it Chris". Then Craig fired his revolver grazing the police officer's shoulder. In spite of being wounded, Fairfax chased Bentley and finally arrested him. Bentley told Fairfax that Craig had a Colt 0.45 revolver and plenty of ammunition.

Meanwhile, reinforcements arrived. A group of police officers went on to the roof. The first policeman to appear on to the roof was Police Constable Sidney George Miles (aged 42). Craig shot him in the head. Miles died. After his ammunition was exhausted, Craig jumped down from the roof on to the road 30 feet below. He fractured his spine and left wrist and was arrested.

Fairfax was awarded the George Cross for his gallantry in pursuing Bentley and Craig. Police Constables Norman Harrison and James McDonald were awarded the George Medal. Police Constable Robert Jaggs was awarded the British Empire Medal. Police Constable Miles was posthumously awarded the Queen's Police Medal for Gallantry.

Even if Craig was found guilty of murder, he could not be sentenced to death because he was only 16 years old - below the minimum age of 18 for execution. But Derek Bentley was over 18 years and could be sentenced to death.

Initially, the case appeared to be a simple, clean and shut case for the prosecution. But as the trial proceeded before Lord Chief Justice Lord

Goddard at the Old Bailey, the prosecution's case appeared far less certain. There were too many missing links. The police was not sure how many shots had been fired-and by whom. A ballistics expert failed to positively identify Craig's revolver as the weapon that had fired the bullet that killed Miles. It was not clear what Bentley meant by the words "Let him have it Chris". Did he mean that Craig should hand over the gun to the officer and surrender? Did he mean that Craig should shoot the officer?

What was clear was that Derek Bentley was illiterate and mentally subnormal. His mental age was only 11. But this fact was never told to the jury. Bentley did not present a 'good image' to the jury. He was mentally ill prepared to undergo cross-examination.

The jury took just 75 minutes to hold both Craig and Bentley guilty of Miles' murder. Due to his age being less than 18 at the time of the offence, Craig was sentenced to detention at Her Majesty's Pleasure. Bentley was sentenced to death.

Appeals highlighting the ambiguous evidence, Bentley's mental age and the fact that he did not fire the fatal shot were filed before the then Home Secretary. All were rejected. On January 28, 1953, Derek Bentley was hanged at London's Wandsworth Prison. Christopher Craig was released after 10 years in prison.

At the time of Bentley's execution, the Home Secretary David Maxwell Fye strongly defended capital punishment. He said there was no possibility of an innocent man being hanged in his country.

Many people in Britain disagreed with him. There were several flaws in the prosecution. Before the trial, the defense team was told that the gun used in the killing was missing, so they could not have it sent for forensic testing. During the trial, the gun was mysteriously found at a police station. A police officer later admitted that the bullet that killed Miles was never found - and that "a proper forensic examination would have proved that Craig had not killed the police officer."

It is generally believed that Miles was accidentally killed by a bullet from a police gun. And one of the police officers on the roof that night later admitted that Bentley had never said, "Let him have it."

Two hundred members of parliament signed a motion for Bentley. On the night of the execution, 5,000 people gathered outside the prison chanting, "Murder!" They fought with the police, tore down and burned the death notice that had been pinned outside the gates.

Largely as a response to the outrage created by the execution of Bentley, a few years later, the British government abolished the death penalty.

Meanwhile, relatives and friends of Bentley continued with their efforts to obtain a posthumous pardon for Bentley. They approached film makers, authors and lawyers and urged them to take up the case. As a result, songs were composed, movies made and books written that made the case widely known. Yet, year after year, the government refused to hold a public inquiry.

In 1991, Kenneth Clark, the Home Secretary, rejected a report by the Metropolitan Police which said that there were "reasonable doubts in this case" for a review.

However, on July 30, 1998, the Court of Appeal overturned the controversial conviction of Derek Bentley. In an unprecedented and damning attack, Lord Chief Justice, Lord Bingham, ruled that his predecessor and Bentley's trial judge, Lord Chief Justice Goddard, had denied Bentley "that fair trial that is the birthright of every British citizen."

In his 52-page judgment, Lord Bingham put the blame for the miscarriage of justice on Lord Goddard. He described Lord Goddard as "blatantly prejudiced"; concluded that Lord Goddard had misdirected the jury; and had in his summing-up put unfair pressure on the jury to convict.

After nearly half a century, the British justice system finally admitted its mistake and granted Bentley a full pardon. Immediately after the pardon, Derek Bentley's surviving relatives - his brother Denis and niece Maria Bentley Dingwall - applied for compensation.

The Home Secretary Jack Straw ruled that Bentley's conviction was overturned on the basis of mistakes by the trial judge. Therefore, the case fell outside the compensation scheme. Straw expressed enormous sympathy for the family but said there were no other "sufficiently exceptional" circumstances leading to his conviction to merit payment of compensation.

On the other hand, Bentleys' solicitors agreed that though strictly speaking, Bentley's case did not fall within the compensation scheme, compensation should be granted under the ex-gratia scheme because there were exceptional circumstances. They said "There can be no more exceptional circumstances than in this case."

The Bentleys were prepared to go to the courts again for compensation. And if necessary, they were prepared to go even to the European Court of Human Rights.

Finally, in an unprecedented move, in May 1999, Home Secretary Jack Straw reconsidered his earlier ruling and agreed to give compensation to the Bentleys.

Pretty: My Lordships. I will now take you through the case of James Hanratty. The conviction and subsequent execution of James Hanratty at Bedford Prison has been regarded as extremely controversial.

On the evening of August 22, 1961, a car containing two lovers Michael Gregsten and Valerie Storie - two civil servants employed at the Road Research Laboratory in Slough, Berkshire - was parked by a field near Slough. A man threatened the couple with a gun. After entering the car's back seat, he ordered Gregsten to drive on. They drove for about 30 miles before the gunman ordered Gregsten to pull in to a lay-by on the A6 road near Bedford.

The stranger then asked for a duffle bag. Gregsten attempted to disarm him. The gunman fired twice from point blank range and killed Gregsten. After that, the gunman raped Valerie Storie and then shot five bullets into her. Thinking that she was dead, he fled. She survived, but was paralyzed for the rest of her live.

The police constructed an Identikit picture of the killer from Valerie Storie's description, but this differed from descriptions provided by other witnesses. So two pictures were prepared and issued. Meanwhile, the police discovered two 0.38 cartridge cases from the hotel room occupied on the night before the murder by Mr. J. Ryan (an alias used by James Hanratty). However, the same room was occupied by Peter Louis Alphon, who was not selected by Valerie Storie from an identity parade.

Hanratty was arrested in Blackpool on October 9, 1961. He was identified by Valerie Storie and sent for trial. The whole trial centred on his identification. Hanratty claimed to have been in Rhyl on the day of the murder - 200 miles away from the murder scene in Bedfordshire.

After deliberating 9½ hours, the jury found Hanratty guilty of the murder of Michael Gregsten. Hanratty was sentenced to death by hanging and was hanged at Bedford Prison on April 4, 1962.

Under the Homicide Act 1957, this was a murder case punishable with death because Michael Gregsten had been shot. If Gregsten had been stabbed, strangled or poisoned to death, then Hanratty could not have been sentenced to death.

There has been a lot of controversy regarding the conviction and execution of James Hanratty. The controversy was mainly concerned with the correct identification of the suspect. The controversy was also about the need to establish beyond reasonable doubt the guilt of a suspect person.

Towards the end of March 1999, the Criminal Cases Review Commission (CCRC) decided to refer the case back to the Court of Criminal Appeal. The Court could then decide whether to quash Hanratty's conviction, or let the conviction stand. But to put the matter beyond doubt, forensic experts needed a sample of DNA from Hanratty's remains which lay buried in a Hertfordshire cemetery.

The Court of Appeal does not have the power to order an exhumation. But the Lord Chief Justice, Lord Woolf, said every step should be taken to establish whether the trial jury was correct when they found Hanratty guilty. He ordered exhumation on the ground that it would be desirable "in the interests of justice".

On March 22, 2001, James Hanratty's remains were exhumed from Bedford Prison, (and later reburied in Carpenter's Park Cemetery, near Bushey in Hertfordshire). A DNA sample was sent to forensic experts for matching with two samples taken from the scene of the crime. The results showed there was a 2.5 million to one chance that the samples came from someone other than Hanratty.

On May 10, 2002, the Court of Criminal Appeal (Lord Chief Justice Woolf, Lord Justices Mantell and Leveson) ruled that Hanratty's conviction was not unsound and that there were no grounds for a posthumous pardon.

Birmingham Six

Pretty: My Lordships. I will take you through the Birmingham Six case. This case does not involve capital punishment. But it does show what would have happened if capital punishment had not been abolished in U.K. Six innocent persons would have been executed.

On November 21, 1974, bombs planted in two central Birmingham pubs - the Mulberry Bush (later renamed, and in 2003 re-developed as a tourist information office); and the Tavern in the Town, a basement pub on New Street (later renamed and now a branch of Pizza Hut) exploded at 20:25 and 20:27 hours. A third bomb planted outside a bank on Hagley Road failed to explode.

The two explosions were the most injurious terrorist blasts in Britain. Twenty one people were killed (ten at the Mulberry Bush and eleven at the Tavern in the Town). 182 people were injured. The bombings were attributed to the Provisional IRA, although two days later, the Provisional IRA denied this.

Six men - Hugh Callaghan, Patrick Hill, Gerard Hunter, Richard McIlkenny, William Power and John Walker were arrested. All the six men were born in Belfast but had lived in Birmingham since the 1960s.

Later, they claimed that five of them, Hill, Hunter, McIlkenny, Power and Walker, had left the city from New Street Station, on November 21, a few hours prior to the explosions, to go to Belfast to attend the funeral of James McDade, an IRA member who had accidentally killed himself while planting a bomb in Coventry. They claimed they were seen off at the New Street Station by Callaghan.

In Heysham, they and others were stopped and searched by the Special Branch. They did not tell the police the true purpose of their visit to Belfast. During the course of this search, the police were informed about the Birmingham bombings and they were taken to Morecambe police station.

On the morning of November 22, after the questioning, the six men were transferred to the custody of West Midlands Serious Crimes Squad police unit and interrogated by Birmingham CID. Callaghan was taken into custody on the evening of November 22. Later, they claimed that over three days of questioning, they were beaten, threatened and forced to sign statements written by the police.

The six men were produced in court on November 25; remanded to custody and taken to Birmingham. They claimed they were subjected to further ill-treatment in the prison.

In June 1975, fourteen prison officers were charged with varying degrees of assault - but were found not guilty

On May 12, 1975 the six men were charged with murder and conspiracy to cause explosions. The trial began in Lancaster, England on June 9, 1975. The accused repudiated their confessions.

However, the statements made by the six men in November were deemed admissible in evidence. The other evidence against them was largely circumstantial - through their association with IRA members. The jury found the six men guilty of murder. On August 15, 1975, they were sentenced to life terms. Their appeal was dismissed in March 1976.

In 1977, the six men pressed charges against the West Midlands police. These charges were dismissed. In 1986, a second appeal was dismissed.

Journalists took up the case as a miscarriage of justice, and over the next five years, a series of newspaper articles, television documentaries and books brought fresh evidence questioning the conviction.

Their third appeal, in 1991, was successful. New evidence of police fabrication and suppression of evidence; the discrediting of both the confessions and the 1975 forensic evidence led to the Crown offering no case against the men. In 2001, compensation ranging from £ 840,000 to £ 1.2 million were awarded to the six men.

The miscarriage of justice resulted in the Home Secretary setting up a Royal Commission on Criminal Justice in 1991. The Commission's report of

1993 led to the Criminal Appeal Act of 1995 and the establishment of the Criminal Cases Review Commission in 1997.

It was Paddy Hill who doggedly fought against the odds and finally obtained reopening of the case, as well as damages for himself as well for the other five persons.

Pretty: My Lordships. I have finished for the day. I thank you all very much.

Justice A: The court is adjourned for the day. We will assemble tomorrow again at 10.30 A.M. sharp.

Capital punishment is as fundamentally wrong as a cure for crime as charity is wrong as a cure for poverty.

> Henry Ford

A jury consists of twelve persons chosen to decide who has the better lawyer.

> Robert Frost

It is the poor, the sick, the ignorant, the powerless and the hated who are executed.

> Attorney Ramsey Clark

Day 2

The media had given extensive coverage to the previous day's proceedings. Every word uttered by Pretty Singh had been lapped up by all the major newspapers and widely broadcast over the T.V. and radio channels.

Back to Supreme Court of India's Court Room No. 1. The time is 10.30 A.M. The scene is much the same as yesterday. The judges are in their seats.

Justice A: You may begin.

Pretty: My Lordships. I will take you through the history of capital punishment in the U.S.

Capital punishment is one of the two most controversial issues in the U.S. - the other issue being abortion. The majority of U.S. citizens, including many Catholics, are in favour of capital punishment.

From time to time, wrong executions have high lighted human fallibility and stirred up controversies. To compound matters, different states have different laws relating to capital punishment. And they have different methods of execution.

Unbelievably, the Americans have executed more persons than any other democratic country in the world. Since 1930, more than 4,500 people have been executed in the U.S. Executions have been treated as local affairs. No central agency has kept records of the executions. There is no way of knowing the exact numbers of those executed. In addition, between 1882 and 1951, there have been 4,730 recorded lynchings by vigilantes.

In 1972, the U.S. Supreme Court struck down state death penalty laws and effectively halted all executions. However, in 1976, after the adoption of new procedures, the U.S. Supreme Court reinstated the death penalty.

On an average, between 1982 and 1999, two hundred and fifty to three hundred and fifty persons have been sentenced to death every year. But in the last few years, the number of death sentences has dramatically dropped. The number of executions has gradually increased as appeals have become exhausted. In 1999, the number reached the all time high 98. 39 persons have been executed in the first eight months of 2007 taking the total number to 1095.

Sometimes, governors and presidents find it difficult to pardon the condemned - even in cases they feel are deserving - due to the pressure of strong public opinion or the fear of political backlash.

Late Pope John Paul II was one of the world's leading advocates for the abolition of capital punishment and frequently spoke in favour of abolition. Just prior to the Pope's arrival in St. Louis, the Missouri Supreme Court unilaterally changed the date of execution of a convicted killer Darrell Mease to a date after the Pope's departure.

In 1999, late Governor Mel Carnahan, who had previously allowed execution of 22 men during his seven years in office as Governor of Missouri, spared the life of Darrell Mease at the specific request of Pope John Paul II during his celebrated trip to St. Louis.

This brief flirtation with mercy became very controversial and cost late Governor Mel Carnahan dear. Newspapers across Missouri published letters bitterly denouncing him for giving in to the Pope.

When he ran for the Senate in 2000, his opponent, incumbent Senator John Ashcroft, continued to make a public issue of the pardon. We do not know what the outcome would have been. Governor Carnahan, his son Randy, and an aide were killed in a plane crash on October 16, 2000.

But some governors, like George Ryan, the Republican Governor of Illinois, take a more dispassionate view. George Ryan had earlier campaigned in support of the death penalty. But later he said, "There is a flaw in the system, without question, and it needs to be studied".

In January 2000, George Ryan issued a moratorium on imposition of the death penalty in Illinois. He reviewed death penalty cases since 1977. He determined that 13 death row inmates in the state had been cleared of murder charges, compared to 12 who had been put to death. Some of the 13 inmates were taken off death row after DNA matching exonerated them. Others were exonerated after new trials were ordered by appellate courts.

Finally, in January 2003, George Ryan commuted all death sentences to prison terms of life or less.

In June 2002, the Supreme Court reversed a ruling it had made 13 years earlier, and by a 6-3 decision held that capital punishment to those who are mentally retarded constitutes "cruel and unusual punishment" to this group. The court relied in part on the degree to which public opinion by then characterized the punishment as excessive. A number of states had already passed legislation prohibiting such executions. As many as 10% of death row inmates in the U.S. suffer from mental retardation.

37 of the 50 U.S. states have death penalty in their laws. The death penalty is also provided under US federal military and civilian law.

On April 1, 2006, over 3,360 convicts were under sentence of death. 53 convicts were executed in 2006. 39 convicts have been executed during the first eight months of 2007 taking the total to 1096 executions since the resumption of the death penalty in 1977.

On March 1, 2005, by a narrow margin, the U.S. Supreme Court reversed an earlier ruling and abolished death penalty for juveniles. Relying on the "cruel and unusual punishment" provisions of the 8th Amendment, the Court cited the overwhelming weight of international opinion as a partial basis for the ruling.

U.S. is a leader in technology and science but certainly backward in terms of penology. While most countries of the Western world have abolished or severely restricted the use of the death penalty,

U.S. has embraced capital punishment more and more fervently.

In 1968, Dr. Karl Menninger, then the most prominent psychiatrist in the U.S., published his book *The Crime of Punishment* opposing capital punishment. Ever since the 1930s, he had said that we should not waste good guinea pigs.

Pretty: My Lordships. During the 1990s, three retired U.S. Supreme Court justices have condemned capital punishment:

In 1991, Lewis F. Powell, Jr., retired Supreme Court Justice, said, "I have come to think that capital punishment should be abolished."

In 1994, Harry Blackmun, retired Supreme Court Justice said, "From this day forward, I no longer shall tinker with the machinery of death. For more than 20 years I have endeavored – indeed, I have struggled – along with a majority of this court, to develop procedural and substantive rules that would lend more than the mere appearance of fairness to the death penalty endeavor. Rather than continue to coddle the court's delusion that the desired level of fairness has been achieved and the need for regulation eviscerated, I feel morally and intellectually obligated to concede that the death penalty experiment has failed."

In 1996, William J. Brennan, Jr., retired Supreme Court Justice, said, "One area of law more than any other besmirches the constitutional vision of human dignity. . . . The barbaric death penalty violates our Constitution. Even the most vile murderer does not release the state from its obligation to respect dignity, for the state does not honor the victim by emulating his murderer. Capital punishment's fatal flaw is that it treats people as objects to be toyed with and discarded. . . . One day the Court will outlaw the death penalty. Permanently."

In December 2007, New Jersey became the first US State since 1965 to repeal the death penalty. The state's move is being hailed all around the world as a historic victory against capital punishment.

Nicola Sacco and Bartolomeo Vanzetti

Pretty: My Lordships. I will take you through one of the earliest controversial executions in U.S. That of Nicola Sacco and Bartolomeo Vanzetti on August 23, 1927.

Sacco and Vanzetti were Italian immigrants who spoke broken English and were anarchists. They were convicted of a payroll robbery in Massachusetts in 1920, during which a paymaster and his bodyguard were shot to death.

At their joint trial, dozens of witnesses testified to their whereabouts at the time of the robbery and murders. Some of the key prosecution witnesses had in the first instance not been able to identify the defendants, but at the trial, were sure of their identifications.

In the seven years between their convictions and electrocutions, a lot of additional evidence surfaced which threw doubt on their guilt. By the time of their executions, the Sacco and Vanzetti case had stirred up a maelstrom of protests not only in the United States, but around the world.

In 1925, Celestine Madeiros – condemned to death in another murder case – confessed to being a member of the gang that committed the robbery for which Sacco and Vanzetti were condemned.

Felix Frankfurter, who was recognized as one of the century's best jurists, wrote a book-length article for *The Atlantic Monthly* that examined Sacco and Vanzetti's case. He concluded their convictions were a travesty of justice and named the probable culprits, a gang of professional robbers. Twelve years after writing this article, Frankfurter was appointed to the United States Supreme Court.

In August 1977, 50 years after the executions, Governor Michael Dukakis of Massachusetts signed a proclamation clearing the names of Sacco and Vanzetti.

Bruno Richard Hauptmann

Pretty: My Lordships. I will now relate the case of Bruno Richard Hauptmann, another controversial case.

On a cold, rainy night of March 1, 1932, between 8:00 and 10:00 o'clock, Charles Augustus Lindbergh III, 20-month old son of Charles Lindbergh - the first aviator to fly solo across the Atlantic - was kidnapped from the second-floor nursery of their home at Hopewell, N.J.

The kidnapper left a ransom note in a small, white envelope on a radiator case near the nursery window. The note read:

> Dear Sir!
> Have 50,000$ redy 2500$ in 20$ bills 1500$ in 10$ bills and 1000$ in 5$ bills. After 2-2 days we will inform you were to deliver the Mony. We warn you for making anyding public or for notify the polise the child is in gute care. Indication for all letters are singnature and 3 holes.

The ransom of $50,000 was paid. The child's battered body was found on May 12, 1932 near Hopewell.

On September 19, 1934, Bruno Richard Hauptmann, a German immigrant, and by profession a carpenter, was found with part of the ransom. In a sensational trial at Flemington, N.J., he was convicted of the kidnapping and murder.

There were only two eyewitnesses at the trial who put Hauptmann near the Lindbergh estate at the time of the crime. It was later revealed one witness had a very bad criminal record; the other was legally blind. The police and prosecution handwriting experts claimed that Hauptmann's writings matched those of the ransom notes. But many other experts have disputed this.

Charles Lindbergh and the man who delivered the ransom money claimed it was Hauptmann who received it. But at the time of the arrest, Lindbergh and the other witness said that Hauptmann was not the man who received the ransom money.

Harold G. Hoffman, Governor of New Jersey, believed Hauptmann was innocent. He believed that the kidnapping could not have been done by one man alone. He secretly visited Hauptmann in his death row cell on the evening of October 16, 1935 with Anna Bading, a stenographer and fluent speaker of German. Under the New Jersey law, Hoffman could not alone commute Hauptmann's term, so Hoffman urged other members of the New Jersey Court of Errors and Appeals (eliminated by the 1947 state constitution) to visit Hauptmann.

Samuel Liebowitz, the defense lawyer in the Scottsboro Boys case, visited Hauptmann's cell three times. Liebowitz tried to convince Hauptmann that his only chance of avoiding the chair was by confessing. A newspaper offered to give Hauptmann's widow, Anna, and young son, $75,000 if he would provide details of his kidnapping to the newspaper.

To the last day, Hauptmann maintained he was innocent; and although temporarily reprieved, he was electrocuted on April 3, 1936.

A number of books have been written on the kidnapping. Some authors have made out a case that some evidence was planted and doctored by the police. There have even been allegations that Lindbergh or a member of his family accidentally killed the child and the kidnapping was staged to cover up that fact.

Lindbergh was an international hero and celebrity. It is said that more journalists covered the kidnapping than covered World War I. The case created great controversy and may never be settled. It led to congressional action against kidnapping.

Scottsboro Boys

Pretty: My Lordships. Most capital punishment cases in the U.S. that have disturbed the public the most are the ones involving white people. I will now relate the case of the Scottsboro Boys.

On March 25, 1931, two white girls, Ruby Bates and Victoria Price, were allegedly gang raped by nine black teenagers on a Southern Railroad freight train passing through Alabama.

Nine black youths - Roy Wright (aged 13), Eugene Williams (aged 13), Andy Wright (aged 17), Haywood Patterson (aged 17), Olin Montgomery (aged 17), Willie Roberson (aged 17), Ozzie Powell (aged 16), Charles Weems (aged 21), and Clarence Norris (aged 21) were charged with and tried for raping these two girls.

During the trial, more than 10,000 outsiders crowded into the small town. More than 100 national guards had to be posted at the courthouse. Prosecutor lawyer Wade Wright addressed the jury with the following inflammatory words, "Now the question in this case is this: Is justice in the case going to be bought and sold in Alabama with Jew money from New York?"

Eight of the youths were convicted. A mistrial was declared in the case of Roy Wright (aged 13) when the jury hung up, with eleven for execution and one for life imprisonment. The eight others were sentenced to death. This resulted in demonstrations in Europe and U.S. Liberal organizations, including the ACLU, NAACP, and International Labor Defense, sprang to the defense. Albert Einstein called for the defendants to be freed.

Eleven months after the arrest of the defendants, Ruby Bates wrote a letter saying that she had not been raped.

In November 1932, the U.S. Supreme Court overturned all of the convictions. On April 9, 1933, Haywood Patterson was retried, convicted and sentenced to death again. On May 7, 1933, thousands of persons marched in Washington in protest of the various trials.

On June 22, 1933, Judge Horton vacated Haywood Patterson's conviction and granted a new trial. The cases were transferred to the jurisdiction of a different judge. In November and December 1933, Haywood Patterson and Clarence Norris were retried, convicted and again sentenced to death.

On July 24, 1937, all charges were dropped against Roy Wright, Eugene Williams, Olen Montgomery and Willie Roberson. On July 5, 1938, the Governor of Alabama commuted the last death sentence, that of Clarence Norris, to life imprisonment.

Eventually, all the Scottsboro Boys, except Haywood Patterson (who escaped from prison in 1948), were paroled from prison. Patterson was later convicted of manslaughter in Michigan following a bar room fight, and died in prison a year later. Clarence Norris, the last living Scottsboro Boy, died on January 23, 1989 at the age 79.

The case of the Scottsboro Boys is remarkable for the number of trials, convictions, reversals and reconvictions involved. It remains a blur on the American judicial system.

Patterson and Norris participated in the writing of two separate books about their lives. Patterson's book, *Scottsboro Boy*, was published in 1950 while he was a fugitive. After its publication, Patterson was arrested by the FBI, but the Governor G. Mennen Williams of Michigan refused Alabama's extradition request. Norris' book, *The Last of the Scottsboro Boys*, was published in 1979. Books have been written and movies made on the Scottsboro Boys.

Caryl Chessman

Pretty: My Lordships. I will relate the case of Caryl Chessman, the case that generated the greatest outcry of all modern cases.

A bandit (nicknamed the Red Light Bandit) would approach victims parked in lonely spots, flash a red light resembling that used by the police, and rob the victims. Sometimes, he would take the woman to another area and rape her.

In January 1948, the Los Angeles police arrested Caryl Chessman (aged 27), a parolee from Folsom Prison, who had spent the better part of his adult life in and out of prison, as the Red-Light Bandit.

Chessman signed a confession, which he later retracted, on the ground that the police had forced him to sign the confession. But eyewitness evidence from the women he had assaulted and a mountain of evidence led to his conviction on seventeen counts, ranging from robbery to kidnapping.

Chessman was indicted under California's Little Lindbergh law, passed in 1933, under which in cases involving kidnapping with bodily harm, the sentence was either life imprisonment without possibility of parole, or death.

The jury accepted the prosecutor's argument that Chessman had committed kidnapping when he moved female victims from the car they were into his car, for the purpose of raping them. The jury did not recommend mercy, so under California's law, the automatic sentence for Chessman was death in the gas chamber.

Chessman did not take any lawyer but represented his case himself. He was a bright man. He studied law while in prison and struggled with the law for twelve long years. He fought his case right up to the U.S. Supreme Court seven times - winning small victories along the way.

Chessman also became a writer, authoring four books. All became very popular. Some were translated into other languages. The first book *Cell 2455:Death Row* became a best seller despite consisting largely of Chessman's idealization of himself as a framed convict and old-fashioned outlaw, who specialized in robbing thieves and defying the law. In this book, he made out a convincing case for his innocence. Several eminent persons from all over the world, including Billy Graham, Eleanor Roosevelt, Robert Frost, Pablo Cassals, Aldous Huxley and thousands others wrote to California Governor Edmund G. "Pat" Brown pleading for mercy for Chessman.

But Brown permitted the execution to proceed. He was tormented by this decision for the rest of his life. Ironically, California subsequently repealed the Little Lindbergh law, and by the time Chessman was executed, kidnapping no longer carried the death penalty.

After the execution, it was revealed that a federal judge had granted Chessman a last-minute reprieve, but the judge's clerk could not pass on the message to San Quentin's warden in time because he had dialled a wrong number minutes before the execution. By that time, cyanide pellets had been dropped and Chessman was executed in San Quentin's gas chamber on May 2, 1960.

Prior to his death, Chessman had claimed that a man named Terranova was the 'Red Light Bandit'. But the Los Angeles police said no such man existed. After Chessman's death, William Bradford Huie (author of *The Execution of Private Slovak*) wrote a story for a popular magazine. Huie claiming that Terranova was an inmate in the Los Angeles County Jail at the time police said he did not exist.

The unusual case, the popularity of his books, his repeated attempts to escape death, the eight stays, the long years of imprisonment, mercy pleas on his behalf from all over the world took the debate on capital punishment to its peak.

Ironically, Edmund G. Brown, the Governor of California, who finally allowed the execution, saying that his hands were tied, was himself an avowed opponent of capital punishment.

Julius and Ethel Rosenberg

Pretty: My Lordships. I will relate the case of Julius and Ethel Rosenberg, a case that generated great outcry at the time and remains one of the greatest controversial capital cases of this century.

Julius and Ethel Rosenberg were convicted of passing atomic secrets to Russia during World War II and sentenced to death for treason. The Rosenberg incident occurred during the McCarthy era – an era when the fear of communism was not only widespread, but near hysteric. The people were forced to sign oaths pledging loyalty. Till the end, the Rosenbergs maintained that they were innocent. They were electrocuted on June 19, 1953 - the first civilians in the history of U.S. to be executed for espionage. There was widespread opposition to their execution.

The Rosenberg case began on February 2, 1950 with the arrest of one Klaus Fuchs, a German-born, U.S.-employed scientist, who confessed to passing secret information on the Manhattan Project, the Allied atomic bomb design venture, to the Soviets. He said he met a Soviet whom he knew only as Raymond.

After the arrest of Fuchs, U.S. authorities began an extensive investigation of Los Alamos, New Mexico - headquarters of the top secret U.S. atomic development programme, where Fuchs worked during the war.

They were specifically looking for Raymond who they identified as the chubby middle-aged chemist, Harry Gold - a Swiss-born chemist. Gold was arrested as an accomplice of Fuchs. The next person to be arrested was David Greenglass, who had worked as a machinist at the Los Alamos atomic testing site during the war.

In July 1950, Greenglass named his sister Ethel Rosenberg and her husband, Julius Rosenberg, an electrical engineer who had worked for the U.S. Army Signal Corps during the war. Both were active members of the Communist Party. Greenglass accused them of convincing him to provide atomic secrets to Harry Gold.

During the trial, which began on March 6, 1951 and ended on March 28, 1951, the Rosenbergs maintained that they were innocent. Greenglass, who had pleaded guilty, testified against his sister and brother-in-law. On April 5, 1951, Judge Kaufman sentenced David Greenglass to 15 years in prison; Harry Gold to 30 years; and he sentenced the Rosenbergs to death.

Despite appeals to higher courts and international pleas for executive clemency, the Rosenbergs were electrocuted at Sing Sing Prison in New York shortly after 8 p.m. on June 19, 1953. Ethel was not killed by the first fifty-seven second jolt of electricity. She was re-strapped to the chair and given two more jolts. She was then pronounced dead. Ethel was the first woman to be executed by the U.S. Government after Mary Surratt was hanged for her role in the assassination of Abraham Lincoln.

Pretty: My Lordships. The Rosenberg trial has been criticized for various reasons. The espionage incident occurred at the height of the "red scare". It is said that the political climate of the time made a fair trial impossible.

Others have questioned the quantum of punishment. Whether the Rosenbergs deserved execution, especially when the only seriously incriminating evidence came from a confessed spy who himself was given a reduced sentence to testify against them.

In June 1950, when the FBI came to question him about Greenglass' accusations, Rosenberg said, "Bring him here – I'll call him a liar to his face."

The only witnesses called by the defense were Julius and Ethel Rosenberg. In reply to all questions concerning their membership in the Communist Party, the Rosenbergs pleaded the Fifth Amendment - most likely to avoid naming other acquaintances who could then have been arrested and prosecuted.

Julius pointed out that he had a modest lifestyle. Had he been a spy, he would have been well paid. But the government's counter argument was that Julius' involvement was not because of monetary considerations. He was motivated by ideological belief. Julius did the work because he was a Communist. Ethel's attitude during the entire trial was perceived as arrogant and contemptuous. Not surprisingly. There was not much evidence against her.

Robert and Michael, the two sons of the Rosenbergs, marched carrying signs reading "Don't Kill My Mommy and Daddy". Protestors picketed. The Pope appealed for mercy. The case had the support of four U.S. Supreme Court Justices, but it required five to save them. Ultimately, the decision came to President Eisenhower. He declined to save the Rosenbergs.

After the fall of the Soviet government, there has been some fresh information. During the 1970s, Khrushchev recorded and published his memoirs. They contain some observations about the role of the Rosenbergs, but not sufficient enough to prove them guilty and warrant a death sentence.

In 1997, Aleksandr Feklisov, Rosenberg's Soviet Superspy described his meetings with Julius between 1943 and 1946. However, he expressed outrage at the injustice meted out to Ethel, who was not engaged in any espionage work.

Nobel Prize winning physicist Harold C. Urey sent a telegram to President Eisenhower a couple of days before execution of the Rosenbergs. He wrote that an army mechanic like David Greenglass was "wholly incapable of transmitting the physics, chemistry and mathematics of the bomb to anyone." In 2001, David Greenglass admitted that the testimony of the Greenglasses relating to Ethel Rosenberg's role in the conspiracy was false. Some experts say that the Rosenbergs did not really pass on any unknown secrets about the bomb to Russia. Even if they did pass on any information, it was useless.

In one of her last letters before being executed, Ethel Rosenberg wrote, "My husband and I must be vindicated by history; we are the first victims of American Fascism."

Pretty: My Lordships. I have finished for the day. I thank you all very much.

Justice A: The court is adjourned for the day. We will assemble tomorrow again at 10.30 A.M. sharp.

Deep below consciousness are other forces, the likes and the dislikes, the predilections and the prejudices, the complex of instincts and emotions and habits and convictions, which make the man, whether he be litigant or judge.

                                                                Benjamin Cardozo

Day 3

The media continued lapping up every word uttered by Pretty Singh. All the major newspapers, T.V. and radio channels covered the court proceedings.

Back to Supreme Court of India's Court Room No. 1. The time is 10.30 A.M. The scene is much the same as yesterday. The judges are in their seats.

Justice A: You may begin.

Pretty: My Lordships. Opponents of the capital punishment argue that the United States is out of step with other industrialized countries in its use of the death penalty. They point out that the only other OECD country which permits the death penalty is Japan, but executions are very infrequent there.

Ronald Cotton

Pretty: My Lordships. I will take you through the case of Ronald Cotton. In July 1984, in two separate incidents, an assailant broke into two apartments, cut phone wires, sexually assaulted two women, searched through their belongings, and took away money and other items.

On August 1, 1984, Ronald Cotton was arrested for the rapes. In January 1985, Cotton was convicted by a jury of one count of rape and one count of burglary.

In a second trial, in November 1987, Cotton was convicted of both rapes and two counts of burglary.

An Alamance County Superior Court sentenced Cotton to life plus 54 years in jail.

Cotton's alibi was supported by family members. The jury was not allowed to hear evidence that the second victim failed to pick Cotton out of either a photo array or a police lineup. The prosecution based its case on several points:

- A photo identification was made by one of the victims.
- Identification was made by one of the victims.
- A flashlight found in Cotton's home resembled the one used by the assailant.
- Rubber from Cotton's tennis shoes was consistent with rubber found at one of the crime scenes.

Cotton's attorney filed an appeal. The North Carolina Supreme Court overturned the conviction because the second victim had picked another man at the identification and the trial court did not allow this evidence to be heard by the jury.

In November 1987, Cotton was retried, this time for both rapes. The second victim had decided that Cotton was the assailant. Before the second trial, a man in prison, who had been convicted for crimes similar to these assaults, stated to another inmate that he had committed Cotton's crimes. The superior court judge refused to allow this information into evidence, and Cotton was convicted of both rapes and sentenced to life.

The next year Cotton's lawyer filed a brief but he did not argue about the judge's failure to admit the second suspect's confession. The conviction was affirmed.

At the request of Cotton's lawyer, in 1994, two new lawyers took over Cotton's defense. They filed a motion for appropriate relief on the grounds of inadequate appeal counsel. They also filed a request for DNA testing that was granted in October 1994. In the spring of 1995, Burlington Police Department turned over all evidence that contained the assailant's semen for DNA testing.

The samples from one victim were too deteriorated to be conclusive. But the samples from the other victim's vaginal swab and underwear were submitted to PCR testing and showed no match to Cotton. At the defense attorney's request, the results were sent to the State Bureau of Investigation's DNA data base containing the DNA patterns of convicted, violent felons in North Carolina prisons. The state's data base showed it matched with the convict who had earlier confessed to the crime.

After Cotton's lawyers received the DNA test results in May 1995, they contacted the district attorney, who joined them in the motion to dismiss the charges. On June 30, 1995, Cotton was officially cleared of all charges and released from prison.

In July 1995, the Governor of North Carolina officially pardoned Cotton. By this time, Cotton had served 10 1/2 years of his sentence. He was eligible for, and the State offered him, $ 5,000 compensation on the basis of a 1948 North Carolina statute which gives $ 500 for each year of wrongful imprisonment up to a maximum of 10 years (which means no compensation beyond 10 years).

Meanwhile, Ronald Cotton is trying to get more compensation and hopes that public attention to his case will persuade the North Carolina legislature to enact a law that could give him and others a substantially higher compensation for wrongful imprisonment.

Kirk Bloodsworth

Pretty: My Lordships. I will take you through the case of Kirk Bloodsworth.

On July 25, 1984, a 9-year-old girl was found dead in a wooded area. She had been beaten with a rock, sexually assaulted, and strangled.

On March 8, 1985, a Baltimore County judge found Kirk Bloodsworth guilty of sexual assault, rape, and first-degree premeditated murder. He sentenced Bloodsworth to death.

The conviction was based on the following evidence:

- An anonymous caller had tipped the police that Bloodsworth had been seen with the girl earlier in the day;
- A witness had identified Bloodsworth from a police sketch compiled by five witnesses;
- The five witnesses had testified that they had seen Bloodsworth with the little girl;

- Bloodsworth had told friends he had done something "terrible" that day that would affect his marriage;
- In his first police interrogation, Bloodsworth had mentioned a "bloody rock" even though no weapons were known of at the time;
- Testimony was given that a shoe impression found near the victim's body was made by a shoe that matched Bloodsworth's size.

In 1986, Bloodsworth's lawyer filed an appeal contending the following:

- Bloodsworth had mentioned the bloody rock because the police had one on the table next to him while they interrogated him;
- The terrible thing mentioned to friends was that he had failed to buy his wife a taco salad as he had promised;
- The police had withheld information from defense lawyers relating to the possibility of another suspect.

In July 1986, the Maryland Court of Appeals overturned Bloodsworth's conviction because of the withheld information. He was retried, and a jury convicted him a second time. This time, Bloodsworth was sentenced to two consecutive life terms. An appeal against the second conviction was denied.

Bloodsworth's lawyer moved to have the evidence released for more sophisticated testing than was available at the time of trial. The prosecution consented. In April 1992, the victim's panties and shorts, a stick found near the murder scene, reference blood samples from Bloodsworth and the victim, and an autopsy slide were sent to Forensic Science Associates (FSA) for DNA testing.

On May 17, 1993, the FSA reported that semen on the autopsy slide was insufficient for testing. It also stated that a small semen stain had been found on the panties. The report indicated that the majority of DNA associated with the epithelial fraction had the same genotype as the semen due to the low level of epithelial cells present in the stain. It was an expected result, according to the report. Finally, the report concluded that Bloodsworth's DNA did not match any of the evidence received for testing. FSA requesteded for a fresh sample of Bloodsworth's blood for retesting in accord with questions about proper labeling on the original sample.

On June 3, 1993, FSA issued a second report that stated its findings regarding Bloodsworth's DNA were replicated and that he could not be responsible for the stain on the victim's underwear.

On June 25, 1993, the FBI conducted its own test of the evidence and arrived at the same results as FSA. In Maryland, new evidence can be presented no later than 1 year after the final appeal. Prosecutors joined a petition with Bloodsworth's attorneys to grant Bloodsworth a pardon. A Baltimore County circuit judge ordered release of Bloodsworth from prison on June 28, 1993.

Maryland's governor pardoned Bloodsworth in December 1993. By this time, Bloodsworth had served almost 9 years of the second sentence, including 2 years on the death row.

Ray Krone

I will relate the case of Ray Krone who was convicted and sentenced to death for sexually assaulting and then killing a waitress in a Phoenix bar in 1991.

On the morning of December 29, 1991, the nude body of thirty-six year old cocktail waitress, Kim Ancona, was found in the men's restroom of the Phoenix, Arizona bar, where she worked.

She had been fatally stabbed. There were no fingerprints. Blood at the scene matched her type. Saliva on her body belonged to someone with the most common blood type. There was no semen.

The only real evidence were bite-marks on the victim's breast and neck. A friend of Kim Ancona told the police that the victim had told her that a regular customer named Ray Krone would help her close the bar the previous night. The police took Krone's teeth impressions on styrofoam for comparison.

On December 31, 1991, Krone was arrested and charged with murder, kidnapping, and sexual assault. Krone had no previous criminal record, had been honourably discharged from the military, and had worked in the postal service for seven years.

Later, experts testified before the court that Krone's teeth impressions on the styrofoam matched those found on Ancona's body. No DNA tests were performed. During his 1992 trial, Krone maintained that he was innocent, and claimed to have been asleep in his bed at the time of the crime. A jury convicted him on counts of murder and kidnapping.

For the two offences, Krone was sentenced to death and twenty-one years of imprisonment. However, Krone was found not guilty of the sexual assault.

In 1996, Krone obtained a new trial in appeal. But once again, he was convicted, mainly on the basis of the expert testimony relating to the bite-marks. However, this time, the judge sentenced Krone to life imprison-ment, doubting whether or not he was the real killer.

Krone's attorney Alan Simpson obtained a court order for DNA testing. In 2002, after Krone had served more than ten years in prison, DNA tests conducted on the saliva and blood found on the victim excluded Krone as the source and instead matched that of another man Kenneth Phillips.

After the DNA testing, the Police admitted that a mistake had been committed; an injustice had been done; that the new DNA findings made it clear that they had the wrong man; and Krone deserved an apology.

On April 8, 2002, Krone was released from prison. On April April 24, 2002, the District Attorney's office filed application to formally dismiss all charges against him.

By this time, Krone had spent 10 years in prison - including two years and eight months in Cellblock 6 in Florence, watching other condemned inmates being taken away for execution.

Ray Krone is the 100th former death row inmate found innocent and freed since the reinstatement of capital punishment in the U.S. in 1976. He is the twelfth death row inmate whose innocence has been proved through post conviction DNA testing.

Orenthal James Simpson

Pretty: My Lordships. I will now relate the case of O.J. Simpson - the most publicized case in the history of U.S. It was the longest trial ever held in California, costing over $20,000,000 to fight and defend, churning up 50,000 pages of trial transcripts.

Eleven lawyers represented Simpson and twenty five lawyers worked round the clock for the largest prosecutor's office in the land. 150 witnesses were examined before a jury that was closeted in the Hotel Intercontinental in downtown Los Angeles from January to October 1995 - for nine months.

Sometime after 10 pm on night of Sunday June 12, 1994, most probably, a single male entered the back entrance of Nicole Brown Simpson's condominium on Bundy Drive in the prestigious Brentwood area of Los Angeles. Nicole Brown Simpson was the former wife of the great footballer and media personality Orenthal James Simpson - O. J. Simpson or simply OJS, as he came to be called.

In a small area near the front gate, the man brutally slashed Nicole, almost severing her neck from the body. Then he struggled with and stabbed 25-year old Ronald Goldman repeatedly - about thirty times. Ronald Goldman was an acquaintance of Nicole's, who had come to return to Nicole a pair of sunglasses her mother had left earlier that evening at the Mezzaluna restaurant where he worked as a waiter.

Just after midnight, the howling of Nicole's dog Akita attracted the attention of a neighbor - Sukru Boztepe. Sukru noticed that Akita had blood on its belly and legs. He followed Akita back to Nicole's house, saw the bodies of Nicole Brown Simpson and Ronald Goldman and asked his wife to phone the police number - 911.

Nicole was no longer married to O. J. Simpson. Yet, the police went to Simpson's home immediately. They found a bloodstain on the door of his white Ford Bronco. They also found a trail of blood leading up to his house. But Simpson was not there.

Actually, Simpson was on board American Airlines flight No. 668 to Chicago. Simpson had taken off from Los Angeles at 11:45 after being driven to the airport in a car chauffeured by Allan Park, an employee of the Town and Country Limousine Company. Park had reported for duty at 10:25, but no one had answered his rings at the door. Park observed a man enter the house at 10:56. He presumed the man to be Simpson. The car had left the Simpson estate about half an hour late.

Police called on Simpson at the O'Hare Plaza Hotel in Chicago on the morning of Monday June 12, 1994. Simpson had come there to attend a convention of the Hertz Rental Car Company. When Simpson was informed that his wife had been murdered, Simpson did not ask how, when, or by whom. According to his later testimony, Simpson had smashed a glass in grief, badly cutting his left hand. However, prosecutors had a different explanation for the injury.

Simpson boarded the next flight to Los Angeles, returning home about noon. He found a full-scale police investigation in progress. Cardboard tags marked bloodstains on the driveway.

That day, Los Angeles police questioned Simpson for about half an hour. They asked Simpson a number of questions about the deep cut on his right hand. However, the officers did not ask obvious follow-up questions.

Eventually, the police accumulated sufficient evidence to connect Simpson with the murders. They obtained an arrest warrant against him. Then they worked out an arrangement with Simpson's attorney, Robert Shapiro, that Simpson would turn himself in at the police headquarters by 10:00 on the morning of June 17 - the day following Nicole's funeral.

Simpson did not turn himself in by the agreed time. The police told Robert Shapiro that they would be driving to Simpson's home to arrest him. Sometime after one o'clock, four officers knocked on Simpson's front door. They found that Simpson had disappeared.

Simpson had left behind a letter addressed to "To whom it may concern". It had the resemblance of a typical suicide letter. The letter ended with the words, "Don't feel sorry for me. I've had a great life, great friends. Please think of the real O. J. and not this lost person. Thanks for making my life special. I hope I helped yours. Peace and love, O. J."

Around 6:20, a motorist in Orange County saw Simpson travelling in the white Bronco of his friend, A. C. Cowlings, and informed the police. A dozen police cars, helicopters carrying newsmen, and some curious members of the public started pursuing the Bronco. The dramatic chase ended with Simpson's arrest in his own driveway. At the time of the arrest, police found $ 8,750 in cash, a false beard and mustache, a loaded gun, and a passport in Cowlings' vehicle.

The trial began on Tuesday, January 24, 1995. Under a drizzling sky, reporters and T.V. crew converged to cover the trial of the century.

Christopher Darden led the prosecution. He portrayed Simpson as an abusive husband and a jealous lover of Nicole Brown Simpson. Over the next 99 days of trial, the prosecution examined 72 witnesses. The first set of witnesses which included relatives and friends of Nicole, friends of O. J., and a 9-1-1 dispatcher, were produced to demonstrate that Simpson had a history of domestic abuse and he had the motive and opportunity to kill.

The prosecution next produced the second set of witnesses which included limousine driver Allan Park, Kato Kaelin and officers of the Los Angeles Police Department - to establish a time table of events that left Simpson with ample opportunity to commit the murders. This suggested that Simpson had in fact used this opportunity to kill his ex-wife and Ronald Goldman.

Finally, the prosecution produced witnesses directly tying Simpson to the two murders. The evidence related to forensic results of blood, hair, fiber, and footprint analysis from the crime scene and Simpson's Rockingham home. The strongest evidence against Simpson were the results of two DNA blood tests.

The first tests indicated that the blood found at the crime scene could have come from only 1 out of 170 million sources of blood - and that O. J. Simpson's blood matched the profile. The second tests came from blood found on two black socks at the foot of O. J.'s bedroom. According to the prosecution, only 1 out of 6.8 billion sources of blood matched the sample and Nicole might well be the only person on earth whose blood matched the blood found on the socks.

During cross-examination of the prosecution's DNA experts, the defense lawyers developed the theory that either the blood samples were contaminated or they were planted by corrupt police officers.

The media termed Simpson's defense team as the "Dream Team". Johnnie Cochran opened the case for the defense. He suggested Simpson was so crippled by arthritis that he could not possibly have committed the two murders. Cochran told the jury that the defense would prove that the evidence against Simpson was contaminated, compromised, and ultimately corrupted.

An important aspect of the case was the evidence of Mark Fuhrman, the police officer who had found the bloody glove. The defense tried to prove that he was a racially biased officer and had planted evidence.

Fuhrman denied using the word "nigger". It later turned out from a tape recorded conversation with Laura Hart McKinny, a journalist, that during a conversation with her, Fuhrman had used the word "nigger" several times. Fuhrman had also disclosed to her that sometimes he had planted evidence to help secure convictions. This made the defense formulate the theory that Fuhrman took a glove from the Bundy crime scene, rubbed it in Nicole's blood, then took it to Rockingham and dropped it outside Kaelin's bedroom so as to frame Simpson.

Fuhrman's testimony damaged the case to some extent. But the testimony of the soft-spoken Chinese-American forensic expert Henry Lee won Simpson his acquittal.

Lee had solid credentials, a winsome smile and provided the jury a plausible support for doubting the prosecution's key forensic evidence. Lee raised doubts about blood splatter demonstrations. He said that shoe print evidence suggested the presence of more than one assailant. About the DNA tests, he simply said, "Something's wrong."

The jury spent only three hours deliberating the case that had produced 150 witnesses over 133 days. 142 million people - an unbelievable 91% of television viewing audience watched the TV and listened on radio as the verdict was delivered at 10 a.m. PST on October 3, 1995. Ito's clerk, Deidre Robertson, announced the jury's verdict: "We the jury in the above entitled action find the defendant, Orenthal James Simpson, not guilty of the crime of murder."

Simpson was acquitted. But after this judgement, Simpson had to face a civil trial in Santa Monica. This trial took just three months and produced a different result. Photos showing Simpson wearing size 12 Bruno Magli shoes that he claimed did not belong to him turned up first in one newspaper, then in others. The judge did not allow Simpson's lawyers to introduce theories of top-to-bottom conspiracy. Applying the preponderance of evidence test applicable to civil cases, the jury held that Simpson had wrongfully caused the death of Nicole Brown Simpson and Ronald Goldman.

The jury ordered Simpson to pay compensatory damages of $8.5 million and punitive damages of $25 million. The Simpson trial laid bare the polarization of racial attitudes on such issues in the U.S.

Pretty: My Lordships. I have finished for the day. I thank you all very much.

Justice A: The court is adjourned for the day. We will assemble tomorrow again at 10.30 A.M. sharp.

At the end of the day, perhaps the best argument against capital punishment may be that it is an issue beyond the limited capacity of government to get things right.

Scott Turow

Day 4

The media had continued giving extensive coverage to the previous day's proceedings. All the major news papers, radio and T.V. channels were reporting the proceedings.

Back to Supreme Court of India's Court Room No. 1. The time is 10.30 A.M. The scene is much the same as yesterday. The judges are in their seats.

Justice A: You may begin.

Pretty: My Lordships. I will now take you through the history of capital punishment in Canada.

In 1865, murder, treason and rape carried the death penalty in Upper and Lower Canada. The first private bill calling for abolition of the death penalty was introduced in 1914. In 1954, rape was removed from the list of capital offences. In 1956, a parliamentary committee recommended exempting juvenile offenders from the death penalty, providing expert counsel at all stages of the proceedings and the institution of mandatory appeals in capital cases.

In 1961, Canadian Parliament classified murder into capital and non-capital offences. Capital murder offences in Canada meant premeditated murder and murder of a police officer, guard or warden in the course of duty. A capital offence carried the mandatory sentence of hanging.

Between 1867 and 1962, there were 710 executions in Canada. The last executions were carried out on

December 11, 1962. Arthur Lucas, convicted of the premeditated murder of an informer and witness in racket discipline, and Robert Turpin, convicted of the unpremeditated murder of a policeman to avoid arrest, were hanged in Don Jail in Toronto, Ontario. Between 1879 and 1960, 438 death sentences were commuted.

Between 1954 and 1963, a private member's bill calling for abolition of the death penalty was introduced in the parliament every year. The first major debate on the issue took place in the House of Commons in 1966. Following a lengthy and spirited debate, the government introduced and parliament passed Bill C-168, which limited capital murder to the killing of on-duty police officers and prison guards.

In 1976, capital punishment was removed from the Canadian Criminal Code and replaced with a mandatory life sentence without the possibility of parole for 25 years for all first-degree murders.

When the motion to reintroduce capital punishment was announced in February of 1987, public opinion polls indicated 73% support for reintroduction. But following widespread discussion on death penalty in the media, by June, when the parliamentary vote was taken, the support had slipped down to an all-time low of 61%. On June 30, the motion was defeated by 148-127 votes.

A national poll conducted in June, 1995 showed that 69% Canadians moderately or strongly favoured return of the death penalty - the same level of support as existed some 20 years ago.

Another opinion poll taken in December of 1998 indicated a dramatic increase in the number of Canadians who opposed the death penalty. The survey which was conducted within two weeks after Canadian Stanley Faulder was granted a last-minute stay of execution in Texas, indicated that 48 % Canadians supported the death penalty, 47% were opposed and 5 % unsure.

Capital punishment continued in the Canadian National Defense Act for serious military offences, including treason and mutiny. However, in practice, for over 50 years, no Canadian soldier has been charged with or executed for a capital crime. In 1998, capital punishment was also removed from the Canadian National Defense Act, bringing Canadian military law in line with civil law in Canada.

Under the terms of the Canada/U.S. extradition treaty, Canada may refuse a request for extradition unless assurance is given that U.S. prosecutors will not seek or impose the death penalty. In a number of cases, in order to obtain the prompt repatriation of murder suspects, U.S. prosecutors have voluntarily agreed not to seek the death penalty.

In 2001, in *United States v. Burns*, the Supreme Court of Canada ruled that in extradition cases, it was constitutionally necessary that "in all but exceptional cases" the Canadian government should seek assurances that death penalty will not be imposed, or if imposed, will not be carried out.

The present Canadian government is opposed to capital punishment and there are no current moves for reinstatement of the death penalty.

The government has rejected calls for a national referendum on the issue.

Pretty: My Lordships. Supporters of the capital punishment have always predicted that the number of murders will substantially increase if capital punishment is not there. But the experience of all countries is otherwise.

The homicide rate in Canada did not increase after abolition of the capital punishment in 1976. In fact, the following year, the murder rate declined slightly from 2.8 to 2.7 per 100,000. Over the next 20 years, the homicide rate fluctuated between 2.2 and 2.8 per 100,000, but the general trend has been clearly downwards.

It 1995, the homicide rate reached a 30-year low (1.98 per 100,000) - the fourth consecutive year-to-year decrease and a full one-third lower than in the year before abolition. In 1998, the homicide rate dipped to below 1.9 per 100,000 - the lowest since the 1960s.

During the decade following abolition, the overall conviction rate for first-degree murder doubled (from under 10% to approximately 20%), supporting the general view that judges and juries will award more convictions, if they are not compelled to award the death sentence.

After abolition of the capital punishment, over 6 Canadian prisoners convicted of first-degree murder have been released on grounds of innocence. Two were in jail for more than 10 years before their innocence was established. They would have been executed if Canada had retained the death penalty.

David Milgaard

Pretty: My Lordships. I will now tell you about the case of David Milgaard.

In 1969, David Milgaard (born 1954) and his two friends, Ron Wilson and Nichol John, took a road trip across the Canadian prairies. Ron Wilson later testified that Milgaard had stolen a flashlight from a grain elevator outside Aylesbury.

While they were in Saskatoon, Gail Miller, a 20 year old nursing student, was found dead on a snow bank. At the time, Milgaard and his friends were stopping to pick up a casual friend Albert Cadrain, whose family was renting out their basement to Larry Fisher, an ex-con who would later be found guilty of the crime.

Cadrain, who admitted he was mostly interested in the $2000 reward for giving the information, tipped off the British Columbia police. Milgaard was arrested in May 1969 and sent back to Saskatchewan where he was charged with Miller's murder.

Cadrain testified that he had seen Milgaard returning on the night of Miller's murder in blood-stained clothing. Cadrain also claimed that Milgaard was also a secret Mafia member who was plotting to have witnesses assassinated.

Both Ron and Nichol also gave evidence against Milgaard. They had originally told the police that they had been with Milgaard the entire day and they believed him to be innocent. But they changed their stories in the court. Ron later retracted his testimony stating that he had been told that he himself was under suspicion and wanted to alleviate the pressure on himself.

On January 31, 1970, exactly a year after Miller's murder, the 16 year old Milgaard was sentenced to life imprisonment. He appealed several times, but the appeals were blocked by the bureaucracy; and by the judicial system which was not receptive to those who were not willing to admit their guilt. Those who did not admit their guilt were considered as lacking in remorse.

Milgaard's formal application was completed in 1988, but was considered in 1991 only after a Liberal MP, Lloyd Axworthy addressed the Parliament:

> "...I wish to speak of a travesty of justice. I speak of the plight of David Milgaard who has spent the last twenty-one years of his life in prison for a crime he did not commit. Yet for the last two years, the Department of Justice has been sitting on an application to reopen his case.... But rather than review these conclusive reports, rather than appreciate the agony and trauma of the Milgaard family, the Minister of Justice refuses to act."

Parliament acted, but rejected Milgaard's application for a Conviction Review. However, in 1992, the Supreme Court of Canada reversed the conviction and ordered a new trial. Finally, on July

18, 1997, DNA evidence cleared Milgaard of the crime.

On July 25, 1997, Larry Fisher was arrested for the murder and rape of Ms. Miller. On May 17, 1999, the Canadian government gave Milgaard compensation of $10 million.

On September 30, 2003, the Canadian government appointed a Royal Commission, headed by Justice Edward P. MacCallum, to investigate Milgaard's wrongful conviction.

David Milgaard case received international attention and is a topic of legal studies today.

Donald Marshall

Pretty: My Lordships. I will tell you about the case of Donald Marshall.

Donald Marshall was sentenced to life imprisonment for murdering his friend Sandy Seale, a Black youth from Whitney Pier on May 28, 1971. They had been walking together in a Sydney, Nova Scotia park, and Seale was attacked by a stranger.

They met two men who started a conversation. One of these men, Roy Ebsary, later described by the Royal Commission of Enquiry Report as "an eccentric and volatile old man with a fetish for knives", fatally stabbed Sandy Seale in the stomach, without any provocation or warning. Sandy died on May 29, 1971.

Donald, only 16 and living in his home on the Membertou reserve, was arrested on June 4, 1971 and charged with non-capital murder. The subsequent events proceeded unthinkably much too fast. The preliminary inquiry was over July 5, 1971 in just one day. His trial was heard over only three days from November 2 - 5, 1971. The entire judicial process was over in this remarkably short time and Donald was sentenced to life imprisonment for a murder he did not commit.

Donald continued with his struggle to free himself and clear his name but he had to spend 11 years in jail before a witness came forward to say he had seen another man stab Sandy. Donald was acquitted by the Nova Scotia Court of Appeal in 1983.

The Government appointed a Royal Commission of Inquiry on the Donald Marshall Jr. Prosecution. The Royal Commission released its much awaited report on the wrongful conviction for murder on January 26, 1990.

The Royal Commission found that the criminal justice system had failed Donald Marshall, Jr. at virtually every turn - from his arrest and wrongful conviction in 1971, up to, and even beyond, his acquittal by the Court of Appeal in 1983; that the conviction occurred because of police and prosecutorial misconduct, the incompetence of his defense counsel, perjured testimony, jury bias and judicial error.

The Royal Commission further found that the fact that Marshall was a Native is one reason why John

McIntyre (the Sydney Police Chief heading the Seale murder investigation) singled him out so quickly as the prime suspect without any evidence to support his conclusion.

The most significant finding of the Royal Commission is that justice in Canada has not been indifferent to colour or social status; that racism played a role in Marshall's imprisonment; and that Donald Marshall Jr. was convicted and sent to prison, in part at least, because he was a Native person.

On February 7, 1990, the Nova Scotia government officially apologized to Donald Marshall Jr. for his wrongful conviction.

Thomas Sophonow

Pretty: My Lordships. I will now tell you about the case of Thomas Sophonow.

In March 1982, Thomas Sophonow was charged with strangling to death waitress Barbara Stoppel (aged 16) in Winnipeg in 1981. Sophonow had to go through three murder trials. The first trial resulted in a hung jury. The second trial produced a conviction which was subsequently set aside. The third trial again produced conviction by jury.

The Manitoba Court of Appeal not only allowed Sophonow's appeal against the last conviction, but instead of ordering another fresh trial, ordered his acquittal. By the time Sophonow was finally acquitted and freed, he had been in custody three years and nine months.

Fifteen years later, in June 2000, the Winnipeg Police Service announced that Sophonow was not responsible for the murder. The Manitoba Attorney General offered public apology to Sophonow and announced a Commission of Inquiry to review the investigation and prosecution of Sophonow to determine whether mistakes were made and whether compensation should be provided. In 2001, the Commission awarded Sophonow compensation of $2.6 million for the four years he had spent in jail.

The Commission of Inquiry found many flaws in the system. They found that investigators focused so much on their prime suspect that they failed to follow up other possible suspects. They found that prosecutors relied heavily on jail house informants. They found that as many as eleven jail house informants were approached by the police and three such witnesses testified against him. They found that those who did testify had charges dropped against them or received other favours. A number of procedural changes have since been made in Ontario.

Terry Samuel Arnold (aged 42), a serial killer, is believed to be the real murderer. Arnold had a long history of violent crime. He was found guilty of the rape of four Newfoundland girls including one just 10 years old. He was also convicted of a murder in Penticton, B.C.

Arnold told the police that he killed a young runaway after she refused to have sex with him. That conviction was later stayed. The body of Arnold was discovered in a Victoria apartment. Police believe Arnold killed himself.

Guy Paul Morin

Pretty: My Lordships. I will now tell you about the case of Guy Paul Morin.

Guy Paul Morin (aged 23), who worked for a furniture manufacturer, lived with his parents in the quiet town of Queensville, southern Ontario. He played the clarinet and saxophone. He was generally happy and looked forward to a bright future.

Christine Jessop (aged 9) and her parents lived next door. On October 3, 1984, Christine's school bus dropped her off at her home. Her parents were not home. When they arrived at around 4:30 pm, they found her backpack on the kitchen counter. The mail and flyers had been brought into the house which meant Christine had arrived home safely. But there was no sign of her. They searched the neighbourhood. Christine could not be found.

Christine's mother, Janet, telephoned the police between 7 and 8 pm. York Regional Police sent emergency vehicles and seventeen police officers, including a police dog and its handlers to the Jessop home over the next seven hours. The police visited Guy Paul Morin's house next door and made routine enquiries.

York Regional Police continued to treat the case as a missing person case until December 31, 1984, when a body was found along Ravenshoe Road in Durham Region, 56 kilometers (33.2 miles) from the Jessop home. On January 1, 1985, dental records identified the body as that of Christine.

The missing case was instantly changed to that of homicide. An autopsy was conducted. The coroner concluded that Christine had been dead for three to four months. It was not known if she had been sexually assaulted.

Morin was questioned about Christine's death on February 22, 1985. He was arrested on April 22, 1985. His beige Honda was seized and sent to the Ontario Centre of Forensic Science in Toronto. At 8 pm that evening, eighty one items were seized as evidence. Guy Paul maintained his innocence throughout a six-hour interrogation. When it was over, he was charged with Christine's murder.

After a change of venue, Guy Paul Morin's trial began in London, Ontario, on January 7, 1986. On February 7, after the jury had deliberated for thirteen hours, he was acquitted. Guy Paul Morin was set free after spending ten months in jail.

There is no prohibition against double jeopardy in Canada's Charter of Rights and Freedoms. The Crown can prefer appeal. And it preferred appeal on the ground that the trial judge had made a fundamental error prejudicing the Crown's right to a fair trial. On June 7, 1987, the Court of Appeal reversed the jury's decision. Guy Paul Morin was arrested again and charged with first-degree murder. Again, he declared his innocence. He filed an appeal with the Supreme Court of Canada. A new trial date was set.

Christine's body was exhumed and sent to the Ontario Centre of Forensic Science. Many discrepancies turned up. The coroner who had originally examined Christine's body had been very lax in his examination and report.

DNA testing in 1995 completely eliminated Guy Paul Morin as Christine's killer. His appeal against his conviction was allowed and he was acquitted. He was freed on January 23, 1995.

An inquiry into Guy Paul Morin's case uncovered evidence of police and prosecutorial misconduct; and of misrepresentation of forensic evidence by the Ontario government's Centre of Forensic Sciences. It was clear that Guy Paul Morin had been framed.

In a TV interview, Guy Paul Morin said he was horrified and infuriated when the jury found him guilty. He couldn't believe what was happening. He couldn't believe that the same police officers who had committed fraud in his case were still on the police force.

Robert Baltovich

Pretty: My Lordships. I will now tell you about the case of Robert Baltovich.

In 1990, the 16 year old Baltovich graduated in psychology from the University of Toronto. Here he met Elizabeth Bain, a fellow student, where they developed a friendship.

On June 19, 1990, Bain told her mother she was going to the campus to "check the tennis schedule". On June 22, her car was found with a large bloodstain in the back seat. Her body was never found.

Baltovich was arrested on November 19, 1990 and charged with first-degree murder. His case continued in the courts for several years. He consistently maintained innocence. His lawyers suggested that the so-called "Scarborough rapist", the name by which the Canadian infamous serial killer Paul Kenneth Bernardo was then known, might be responsible for the murder.

On March 31, 1992, Baltovich was convicted of second-degree murder. His lawyers appealed. Pending disposal of the appeal, Baltovich was released on bail on March 31, 2000. In September 2004, his appeal was finally processed and his case gained national attention again when his lawyers alleged that he had been wrongfully convicted and that another person Paul Kenneth Bernardo, identified as the Scarborough rapist, was guilty of Bain's murder. They alleged that circumstantial evidence suggested links to Bernardo, and this evidence could not have been available during Baltovich's original trial as the identity of the Scarborough rapist was then unknown.

On December 2, 2004, the Ontario Court of Appeal ordered a new trial for Baltovich.

Paul Kenneth Bernardo (he later assumed the name Paul Teale) (born August 27, 1964) was a Canadian criminal, known for the murders he and his wife Karla Homolka committed.

On June 15, 1991, Bernardo kidnapped fourteen-year-old Leslie Mahaffy, whom he raped and murdered. Her body was found in Lake Gibson near St. Catharines, Ontario.

On April 16, 1992, Bernardo and his wife Homolka, kidnapped Kristen French from a church parking lot. Again, Bernardo raped and murdered her. Later that year, Bernardo started physically abusing Homolka. As a result, she left him in January 1993.

In return for a plea bargain (twelve years in prison) which received a lot of criticism, Homolka agreed to testify against Bernardo in his murder trial which took place in 1995.

During Bernardo's trial for the murders of French and Mahaffy, recordings of the rapes that Bernardo and Homolka had themselves filmed were produced (these have since been destroyed).

On September 1, 1995, Bernardo was convicted of the two murders and sentenced to life imprisonment. Bernardo was also declared a "Dangerous Offender", which means that he will never be released on parole.

Bernardo committed a number of other rapes in the Scarborough, Ontario area, which gave him the nickname "Scarborough Rapist". He is also suspected of having committed other murders.

Pretty: My Lordships. I have finished for the day. I thank you all very much.

Justice A: The court is adjourned for the day. We will assemble again tomorrow at 10.30 A.M. sharp.

The discretion of a judge is the law of tyrants; it is always unknown; it is different in different men; it is casual, and depends upon constitution, temper and passion.

In the best it is oftentimes caprice; in the worst, it is every vice, folly and passion to which human nature can be liable.

Lord Camden

Day 5

The media continued giving extensive coverage to the previous day's proceedings.

Back to Supreme Court of India's Court Room No. 1. The time is 10.30 A.M. The scene is much the same as yesterday. The judges are in their seats.

Justice A: You may begin.

Pretty: My Lordships. I will now take you through the history of capital punishment in Australia.

Between 1829 and 1855, executions of convicted criminals took place in various localities including York, Perth, Fremantle and Canning River. In some cases, the convicts were executed at the very spot where they had committed the crime.

In the nineteenth century, many prisoners were hanged every year - not only for such serious crimes as murder and manslaughter; but even for such petty crimes as burglary, sheep stealing, forgery, sexual assaults and even in one case, being illegally at large.

- Queensland was the first state to abolish capital punishment in 1922. The last execution in Queensland took place in 1913.
- New South Wales abolished capital punishment in 1955. The last execution in New South Wales took place in 1940.

- Tasmania abolished capital punishment in 1968. The last execution in Tasmania took place in 1946.
- The Australian Capital Territory abolished capital punishment in 1973. No executions were recorded.
- The Northern Territory abolished capital punishment in 1973. The last execution in the Northern Territory took place in 1952.
- Victoria abolished capital punishment in 1975. The last execution in Victoria (and Australia) took place in 1967.
- South Australia abolished capital punishment in 1976. The last execution in South Australia took place in 1964.
- Western Australia was the last state to abolish capital punishment in 1984. The last execution in Western Australia took place in 1964.

Australia officially abolished capital punishment throughout the country in 1973. The Death Penalty Abolition Act was passed in 1973 and came into effect on September 18, 1973 - the day it received the Royal Assent. The Abolition Act states "a person is not liable to the punishment of death for any offence".

Lindy Chamberlain Creighton

Pretty: My Lordships. I will relate the case of Lindy Creighton Chamberlain. This case is one of Australia's most publicised murder trials.

Lindy Chamberlain Creighton was convicted of killing her baby daughter Azaria. The conviction was overturned in appeal.

Lindy Chamberlain was born in New Zealand and moved to Australia with her family in 1949. She married Michael Chamberlain, a clergyman and co-follower of the Seventh-day Adventist Church, on November 18, 1969.

Michael and Lindy Chamberlain had two sons - Aidan (born October 2, 1973) and Reagan (born April 16, 1976). Their first daughter, Azaria, was born on June 11, 1980. Michael and Lindy Chamberlain took their three children on a camping trip to Uluru. On the night of August 17, 1980, Lindy reported that Azaria had been taken from her tent by a dingo. A massive search was organised, but Azaria's body was never found.

Although the coroner's inquiry supported Lindy's account of Azaria's disappearance, Lindy was prosecuted for the murder of her child on the basis of the finding of the baby's jumpsuit and of blood found in their car. Lindy was convicted of murder on October 29, 1982 and sentenced to life imprisonment.

Shortly after her conviction and going to jail in Darwin Prison, on November 17, 1982, Lindy gave birth to her fourth child, Kahlia. In February, 1984, the High Court rejected her appeal against her conviction.

Several items of Azaria's clothing were found in February 1986. On the basis of this evidence, Lindy's life sentence was remitted by the Northern Territory Government. A Royal Commission was set up in 1987. The Commission found her innocent. Her conviction was overturned in September, 1988.

A third inquest was held. Although John Lowndes, Northern Territory Coroner, could not determine the cause and manner of the disappearance and presumed death of Azaria, on December 13, 1995, in a 107 page decision, he again cleared Lindy of all convictions.

In 1990, Lindy published *Through My Eyes: an autobiography*. She divorced Michael Chamberlain in 1991 and married Rick Creighton on December 20, 1992. In May 1992, the Government gave her compensation of $1.3 million.

Ronald Ryan

Pretty: My Lordships. I will now relate the case of Ronald Joseph Ryan, a very controversial case. He is the last person to be executed in Australia. His execution created tremendous public outrage leading to the abolition of the capital punishment in Australia.

Most Australians believe that Ronald Joseph Ryan's hanging was a political decision. Ryan just became a pawn in Victorian State Premier Sir Henry Bolte's political career. In the process, a helpless individual got caught in the very powerful game of politics.............and lost.

Ryan was a gambler and small-time crook with no record of violence. In 1964, he was sentenced to 13 years imprisonment for shop-breaking and weapons offences. In those days, prison sentences were very long, even for small offences.

On December 19, 1965, after remaining in Pentridge Prison in Melbourne for 17 months, Ryan and Peter

John Walker (another prisoner) decided they had had enough and decided to escape.

During the escape, George Hodson, a prison guard was shot dead. The police accused Ryan of murdering Hodson and launched a massive campaign against him. After nineteen days on the run, Ryan and Walker were captured in Sydney and extradited back to Melbourne.

Ryan was charged with the murder of George Hodson. In spite of inconsistencies in the evidence, based on circumstantial evidence, on March 30, 1966, Ryan was found guilty. The 12-men jury originally wanted to find Ryan not guilty. But two jurors (who thought capital punishment had been abolished in Victoria) were convinced of Ryan's guilt and persuaded the others to deliver a guilty verdict. Justice John Starke sentenced Ryan to death. Justice Starke found Walker guilty of manslaughter and sentenced him to 25 years imprisonment.

There had not been a single execution in the state of Victoria for the past sixteen years. Since 1951, death sentences of all 35 prisoners (some convicted of heinous crimes) had been commuted to life imprisonment. Everyone thought that Ryan's death sentence would be commuted to life imprisonment.

But when it became evident that Ryan would really be executed, seven members of the trial jury circulated a secret eleventh-hour plea to save Ryan. Four members of the jury signed separate petitions for reprieve. The pleas were ignored and suppressed.

In her last letter to Bolte, Ryan's old mother Cecilia pleaded for Ryan's life. She pleaded that if this request was not acceded to, her son's body should be handed over to her so that she could bury him in dignity. "I plead again for the life of my son, and I ask that even at this late hour you will reverse your decision to hang my son. If you cannot find it in your heart to grant this request, then I pray you will grant me one last favour, that the body of my son be given into my custody immediately after his death. I pray to God for the success of this last prayer and that is, that it find favour." A state official replied to Cecilia, "Your son's life will not be spared, and his body will not be returned to you."

Premier Sir Henry Bolte rejected all appeals and petitions. Ryan was hanged at 8.00 am on Friday, February 3, 1967 in Pentridge Prison. His body was buried and covered with lime within Pentridge Prison in an unmarked grave. The exact location of Ryan's grave has never been disclosed.

Dr. Philip Opas, QC (now aged 91), who was defending Ryan, was then at the height of his law career. After Ryan was hanged, Dr. Opas resigned from the Bar in antipathy and still regrets why he could not save Ryan. Dr. Opas has said that nothing will ever convince him that Ryan was guilty of the murder of Hodson. He claims he will go to his grave firmly believing in Ryan's innocence. Incidentally, Dr. Opas was a supporter of the death penalty, until the day the State of Victoria executed an innocent man.

Coming to the actual evidence, during the escape, Ryan had seized a prison M1 carbine gun. When

Ryan took the carbine, it was loaded with eight rounds. Seven were accounted for. If the eighth round could be accounted for, then Ryan could not have killed Hodson. Moreover, there is no evidence that the gun was fired even once.

The vital witness on this aspect was Helmut Lange, the prison guard in the tower at Pentridge from which Ryan seized the carbine. Lange admitted finding the missing bullet on the floor of a prison guard tower. He had made an official report to prison authorities at the time, attaching the missing bullet. But Lange had been ordered by 'someone' to make a new statement, excluding any reference to the missing bullet. Fearing for his job, Lange made a new statement. Deeply hurt by Ryan's execution, in April 1969, Lange committed suicide by shooting himself in the head while on duty at Pentridge Prison.

The entry and exit points of Hodson's fatal wound clearly indicated that the fatal shot had been fired from an elevated position which meant that Hodson had been shot from a height. But at that point of time, Ryan was on the ground. Mysteriously, neither the cartridge, nor the fatal bullet which passed through Hodson's body, were ever recovered.

In 1986, nineteen years after Ryan's execution, Douglas Pascoe, a prison guard who was on duty at the Number 3 prison guard tower during the escape, confessed on television to firing at Ryan. He believed that his shot may have accidentally killed Hodson. Pascoe claims he did not say anything about it at the time, fearing that he might get into trouble. During the trial, he remained silent, believing that Ryan's death sentence would be commuted to life, and that Ryan would not be executed. But Pascoe's confession was quickly discredited by prison authorities, immediate cover-ups were made, and Pascoe's claim was never officially investigated.

Several days before the execution, four prisoners came forward claiming Ryan had not fired the fatal bullet, but another prison guard from another prison guard tower.

All independent eye-witnesses testified to hearing only one shot being fired. A very excitable prison guard Robert Paterson, gave evidence that during the time of the escape, he came out of the main gate of Pentridge Prison armed with a M1 carbine, identical to the one taken by Ryan. Paterson had made three conflicting statements. In the first he said he heard only one shot. In the other two, he said he heard two shots. He was the only witness who heard two shots.

Ryan was executed, but his execution led to the abolition of the capital punishment in Australia.

Pretty: My Lordships. I have finished for the day. I thank you all very much.

Justice A: The court is adjourned for the day. We will assemble again on the coming Monday at 10.30 A.M. sharp.

During the year 2007, the world continued to move closer to universal abolition of the capital punishment.

By the end of the year 2007:

- 135 countries were total abolitionists - in law or practice.
- 91 countries had abolished the death penalty for all crimes.
- A further 11 countries had abolished it for all but exceptional crimes, such as wartime crimes.
- At least 33 countries were abolitionist in practice. They had not carried out any executions for the previous 10 years or more and were either believed to have an established practice of not carrying out executions or had made an international commitment not to do so.
- 62 other countries and territories had retained the death penalty; but not all of them passed death sentences and most did not carry out executions during the year.

Amnesty International

I have reached the conviction that the abolition of the death penalty is desirable.
Reasons:
(1) Irreparability in the event of an error in justice;
(2) detrimental moral influence on (the people/ societycarrying out an execution).

Albert Einstein

Day 6

The media continued giving extensive coverage to the proceedings.

Back to Supreme Court of India's Court Room No. 1. The time is 10.30 A.M. The scene is much the same as on friday last. The judges are in their seats.

Justice A: You may begin.

Pretty: My Lordships. I will now take you through the efforts made by Amnesty International - the largest non government organization in the world - towards the total abolition of capital punishment.

Amnesty International (AI) is based in London. It was founded by late Peter Benenson, a London advocate, in May 1961.

A news report of two Portuguese students sentenced to seven years' imprisonment for raising a toast to freedom in a Lisbon cafe during the Salazar dictatorship horrified British lawyer Peter Benenson.

Benenson wrote an article "The Forgotten Prisoners" which was published by the British newspaper "The Observer", in its Weekend Review section on May 28, 1961.

His article began, "Open your newspaper - any day of the week - and you will find a report from somewhere in the world of someone being imprisoned, tortured or executed because his opinions or religion are unacceptable to his government. The newspaper reader feels a sickening sense of impotence. Yet if these feelings of disgust all over the world could be united into common action, something effective could be done."

Not content with just one campaign for one country, Benenson wanted to draw the attention of the public every where to the plight of political and religious prisoners throughout the world. Benenson requested "The Observer" to run an international campaign to bombard authorities around the world with protests about the "forgotten prisoners". This was the basis of his articles in "The Observer", which took the shape of a series of letters published as "Appeal for Amnesty".

Benenson coined the term "prisoner of conscience" which soon became a commonly accepted term; and the movement's logo, a candle surrounded by barbed wire, became a worldwide symbol of hope.

Within a month, more than a thousand readers had sent letters of support, offers of practical help and details of many more "Prisoners of Conscience". Within six months, the simple publicity effort had developed into a permanent, international movement. Within a year, the new organization - Amnesty International - had sent delegations to four countries to make representations on behalf of prisoners and had taken up 210 cases. Its members had organized national bodies in seven countries.

Over the years, what began as opposition to the death penalty for political and religious reasons, spread its wings to include every kind of death sentence.

According to Amnesty International, the death penalty is the ultimate cruel, inhuman and degrading punishment. Amnesty International is fighting for total abolition of the death penalty for the following reasons:

- It violates the right to life.
- It is irrevocable and can be inflicted on the innocent.
- It has never been shown to deter crime more effectively than other punishments.

Amnesty International is working for the total abolition of the death penalty by regularly monitoring developments, collecting information and organizing an on-going program of work against the death penalty in cooperation with other human rights organizations and governments throughout the world. Amnesty International collects and publishes latest information and news related to capital punishment (and other human right violations) and maintains a library of reports on death penalty worldwide.

Amnesty International is a member of the World Coalition against the Death Penalty - a coalition that unites national and international human rights organizations, bar associations, trade unions and local and regional authorities in an effort to rid the world of the death penalty.

In 1971, the International Council, decision-making body of the Amnesty International, requested the United Nations and the Council of Europe (European Union) to make every possible effort to achieve total abolition of the death penalty throughout the world.

In 1977, Amnesty International convened an international conference on the death penalty in Stockholm. In 1977, Amnesty International's efforts were recognized by the international fraternity. It was awarded the Nobel Peace Prize in recognition of its fight against injustice. In 1978, Amnesty International was honoured with a United Nations Human Rights Award. In 1989, it organized a worldwide campaign against the death penalty.

Every year, since 1997, the United Nations Commission on Human Rights has passed a resolution calling on countries that have not abolished the death penalty to establish a moratorium on executions.

In 2000, Amnesty International, together with the Community of Sant'Egidio and Sister Helen Prejean of the Moratorium 2000 Project, presented more than three million signatures to United Nations Secretary-General Kofi Annan supporting a moratorium on the death penalty with a view to total abolition worldwide.

On September 14, 2000, Giuliano Amato, Prime Minister of Italy, commented on a scheduled execution in Virginia USA. "The death penalty is disgusting, particularly if it condemns an innocent. But it remains an injustice even when it falls on someone who is guilty of a crime."

The United Nations resolution, adopted in April 2004, was co-sponsored by 76 member states, one more than in 2003 and the highest number ever. Today, 91 member-states of the U.N. are totally abolitionist; 8 are abolitionist for ordinary crimes; 5 are observing a moratorium; 39 are de facto abolitionist (they have not executed anyone for more than ten years); while there are only 49 that maintain the death penalty.

Peter Benenson died onFebruary 26, 2005 at John Radcliffe Hospital in the city of Oxford at the age of 83. Today, Amnesty International has become the world's largest independent human rights organization with more than 1.8 million members and supporters in over 150 countries. Amnesty International is campaigning to abolish the death penalty all over the world.

The progress over the years has been phenomenal. When Amnesty International convened the International Conference on the Death Penalty in Stockholm, Sweden, in 1977 - only 16 countries had abolished capital punishment for all crimes. Today the figure stands at 135.

Pretty: My Lordships. Amnesty International's latest information shows that:

- a total of 135 countries - or more than half the countries in the world - have abolished the death penalty in law or practice.
- 91 countries and territories have abolished the death penalty for all crimes;
- 11 countries have abolished the death penalty for almost all crimes.There are a few exceptions, like wartime crimes;
- 33 countries are abolitionist in practice. They have retained the death penalty in their legislations. But they have not carried out any

execution for the past 10 years or more and are believed to have a policy or established practice of not carrying out executions;
- 62 other countries and territories have retained and use the death penalty, but the number of countries which actually execute prisoners in any one year is much smaller.

The trend worldwide is towards total abolition. Since 1990, over 42 countries have abolished the death penalty for all crimes. They include the following countries:

- in Africa - recent examples include Côte d'Ivoire, Senegal;
- in the Americas - Canada, Paraguay;
- in Asia and the Pacific – Bhutan, Nepal, Phillipines, Samoa, Turkmenistan; and
- in Europe and the South Caucasus - Armenia, Bosnia-Herzegovina, Cyprus, Greece, Serbia and Montenegro, Turkey.
- Uzbekistan, the 135th country in the list of abolitionist countries, has abolished the death penalty from 1 January 2008.

Once abolished, the death penalty has been seldom reintroduced. Since 1985, over 50 countries have abolished the death penalty in their law; or, having previously abolished it for ordinary crimes, have gone on to abolish it for all crimes. During the same period, only four abolitionist countries reintroduced the death penalty. One of them - Nepal - has abolished the death penalty again. Another, the Philippines, resumed executions, but later stopped. There have been no executions in the other two (Gambia, Papua New Guinea).

During 2006, at least 1591 prisoners were executed in 25 countries and 3,861 people were sentenced to death in 55 countries. These figures include only cases known to Amnesty International; the true figures are certainly higher.

Amnesty International is of the view that the death penalty does not have any special deterrent effect. According to it, scientific studies have consistently failed to come up with convincing evidence that the death penalty deters crime more effectively than other punishments. The most recent survey of research findings on the relation between the death penalty and homicide rates, conducted for the United Nations in 1988 and updated in 2002, concluded: ".......it is not prudent to accept the hypothesis that capital punishment deters murder to a marginally greater extent than does the threat and application of the supposedly lesser punishment of life imprisonment."

Amnesty International is of the view that abolition of the death penalty does not increase the homicide rates. According to it, a study conducted for the United Nations in 1988 and updated in 2002 stated: "The fact that the statistics continue to point in the same direction is persuasive evidence that countries need not fear sudden and serious changes in the curve of crime if they reduce their reliance upon the death penalty".

Recent crime figures from abolitionist countries fail to show that abolition has harmful effects. In Canada, for example, the homicide rate per 100,000 population fell from a peak of 3.09 in 1975, the year before the abolition of the death penalty for murder, to 2.41 in 1980, and since then it has declined further. In 2003, 27 years after abolition, the homicide rate was 1.73 per 100,000 population, 44 per cent lower than in 1975 and the lowest rate in three decades.

Amnesty International is of the view that as long as the death penalty is maintained, the risk of executing an innocent person can never be eliminated.

Kenny Richey

Pretty: My Lordships. I will now take you through the case of Kenny Richey.

In 1981, Kenny Richey (aged 18), left his home in Scotland to join his American father in Ohio State. After five years in the States, Kenny decided to return to Scotland.

One week before his departure, in the wee hours of June 30, 1986, a fire broke out in an upper apartment of the building where Kenny and his father lived. The fire spread rapidly, engulfing the living room and hallway before firemen could extinguish the blaze. Two year old Cynthia Collins, who was in the apartment, died from smoke inhalation.

Hope Collins, the divorced mother of Cynthia, had left her apartment after midnight, intending to spend the night with her boy friend. Hope Collins regularly left Cynthia unattended, sometimes giving her adult doses of sleeping pills before leaving. A neighbour had reported this to Putnam Child Welfare Services who had repeatedly contacted Hope about this practice, but no action was taken.

Hope Collins, a friend of Kenny Richey, later claimed that she had left Kenny in charge of the child whilst she went out for the evening. Kenny claimed that he had refused to baby-sit for Cynthia because he was too drunk. Kenny Richey was arrested and tried for the murder.

During the trial, the prosecution's case was that the murder was premeditated, that Kenny had stolen cans of petrol from the greenhouse, climbed onto the shed roof and through the window into the flat. He had disabled the smoke alarm, splashed the flammables onto the carpets and set the flat alight before fleeing. His alleged motive was to harm his ex- girlfriend and her partner who lived in the flat below.

Kenny's court appointed lawyer, William Kluge, had only a couple of years experience and had never handled a capital punishment case. He was not competent to defend Kenny. He did not properly question prosecution evidence, hire experts or allow Kenny to testify. Kenny Richey was convicted of aggravated murder and sentenced to death.

In March 1997, new evidence that could establish Kenny Richey's innocence was presented to Ohio Court of Common Pleas. The evidence conclusively proved that Kenny Richey was innocent. In brief the evidence proved that:

- The forensic tests that had initially been carried out on the carpet were proved to be wholly unreliable.
- New tests performed by America's leading scientists showed that the carpet didn't

contain any ignitable substances at all, and also that the characteristics left by the fire in the flat were not consistent with arson but with an accident.

But this evidence was not admissible because it should have been brought up at the earlier trials.

The state prosecution did not dispute the accuracy of the new evidence. Prosecution lawyer, Dan Gershutz said, "Even though this new evidence may establish Mr. Richey's innocence, the Ohio and United States constitution nonetheless allow him to be executed because the prosecution did not know that the scientific testimony offered at the trial was false and unreliable."

Without giving any reasons, Judge Michael Corrigan (who was the foreman of a panel of three judges who had earlier convicted Kenny and then sentenced him to die by electrocution) agreed and refused the request for an evidentiary hearing and dismissed Kenny's appeal. Thus Kenny was denied the right to prove his innocence of the crime for which was convicted.

On January 25, 2005 the case has been reversed. Had Kenny accepted any of the plea-bargains that he had been offered earlier, by now he would have been released.

Pretty: My Lordships. I have finished for the day. I thank you all very much.

Justice A: The court is adjourned for the day. We will assemble again tomorrow at 10.30 A.M. sharp.

It is the deed that teaches, not the name we give it.

Murder and capital punishment are not opposites that cancel one another, but similars that breed their own kind.

George Bernard Shaw

Day 7

Back to Supreme Court of India's Court Room No. 1. The time is 10.30 A.M. The scene is much the same as yesterday. The judges are in their seats.

Justice A: You may begin.

Pretty: My Lordships. I will now tell you what the United Nations is doing about the abolition of capital punishment.

Throughout the course of history, rulers and governments in various parts of the world have used capital punishment to punish criminals. Crimes which carried the capital punishment have varied from time to time; and ranged from theft to murder. Today, only 62 countries and territories have retained the right to use the death penalty.

The United Nations was formed after the Second World War to prevent unnecessary death and widespread human rights violations which had taken place during the two World Wars.

The Charter of the United Nations and the Universal Declaration of Human Rights laid down the foundations of a new body of laws relating to human rights violations.

The United Nations has gradually expanded the law relating to human rights to encompass specific standards for women, children, disabled persons, minorities, migrant workers and other vulnerable groups, who now possess rights that protect them from discriminatory practices that had long been common in many societies. Virtually every body and specialized agency of the United Nations is involved in the protection of human rights to some degree.

The Charter of the United Nations was signed on June 26, 1945, in San Francisco, at the conclusion of the United Nations Conference on International Organization; and came into force on October 24, 1945. All Member States of the United Nations, including the U.S., are bound by these provisions.

The Charter of the United Nations contains provisions relating to human rights - but only in general terms. Article 55 of the Charter charges the United Nations "to promote universal respect for, and observance of, human rights and fundamental freedoms for all without distinction as to race, sex, language, or religion". Article 56 charges each Member State to help the United Nations to achieve the goals set forth in Article 55.

One of the greatest achievements of the United Nations is the creation of a comprehensive body of human rights law for the first time in history, which provides us with a universal and internationally protected code of human rights, one to which all nations can subscribe and for which all people can aspire.

The United Nations has defined a broad range of internationally accepted human rights - economic, social and cultural, political and civil rights. It has also established mechanisms with which to promote and protect these rights and to assist governments in fulfilling their responsibilities.

The first serious attempt to abolish the death penalty, or at least greatly curtail its use, by the international community, was made in 1948. In what can be termed a historic act, on December 10, 1948, the General Assembly of the United Nations adopted and proclaimed the Universal Declaration of Human Rights. The Universal Declaration of Human Rights was drafted by the United Nations Commission on Human Rights in 1947 and 1948. The Universal Declaration was adopted by the General Assembly of the United Nations on December 10, 1948.

The Universal Declaration of Human Rights defines the rights and freedoms of individuals in greater detail. Article 3 of the Universal Declaration states that "Everyone has the right to life, liberty and security of person". Under Article 5 "No one shall be subjected to torture or to cruel, inhuman or degrading treatment or punishment".

The General Assembly of the United Nations called upon all Member States to publicize the text of the Universal Declaration and "to cause it to be disseminated, displayed, read and expounded principally in schools and other educational institutions, without distinction based on the political status of countries or territories."

Since the Universal Declaration's ratification in December 1948, 135 States have abolished the death penalty, either in law or in practice, and many Member States are encouraging others to abolish it as well.

A Declaration is a non-binding treaty - a sort of expression of intent. But a Convention or a Covenant is a legal instrument. After the Universal Declaration on Human Rights was ratified, some Member States feared that despite its moral force, many countries would not sincerely follow the regulations defined by it.

The General Assembly of the United Nations therefore adopted the International Covenant on Civil and Political Rights (ICCPR) on December 16, 1966. The Covenant strongly encourages all Member States to abolish the death penalty, but allows imposition of the death sentence only for the most serious crimes (Article 6(2)). The Covenant also created the Human Rights Committee - a monitoring body - to oversee the implementation of the Covenant.

The Covenant was to come into effect ten years later. Sufficient number of states became parties to the ICCPR and therefore, the Covenant took effect on March 23, 1976 as planned. It now has 160 ratifications.

The U.S. Senate ratified the ICCPR in June 1992 but made certain exceptions to this treaty. Amongst the exceptions are the provisions that the human rights recognized by this treaty shall not be enforceable in courts in the U.S. *The U.S. Senate has thereby denied its citizens the legal right to secure and enforce the human rights recognized by this international covenant.*

On December 15, 1989, the General Assembly of the United Nations adopted the Second Optional Protocol to the International Covenant on Civil and Political Rights, aimed at the abolition of the death penalty.

The Second Optional Protocol, which entered into force in 1991, was created because many Member States believed that "abolition of the death penalty contributes to enhancement of human dignity and progressive development of human rights" (Preamble to the Second Optional Protocol).

The Second Optional Protocol says "No one within the jurisdiction of a State Party to the present Protocol shall be executed. Each State Party shall take all necessary measures to abolish the death penalty within its jurisdiction" (Article 1).

The Second Optional Protocol allows use of the death penalty during wartime and within justifiable reason. Provision may be made "....for the application of the death penalty in time of war pursuant to a conviction for a most serious crime of a military nature committed during wartime" (Article 2(1)).

The Second Optional Protocol also requires Member States to submit reports to the Human Rights Committee on "measures that they have adopted to give effect to the present Protocol" (Article 3). 60 states have ratified this Protocol.

The United Nations adopted the Convention on the Rights of the Child on November 20, 1989. This came into force on September 2, 1990. Under this Convention, persons below the age of 18 who have committed a crime, commonly known as child offenders, are exempt from capital punishment.

Article 37 of the Convention states: "Neither capital punishment nor life imprisonment without possibility of release shall be imposed for offences committed by persons below eighteen years of age." The Convention, ratified by more than 192 countries, is "the most universally accepted human rights instrument in history". However, two countries - Somalia and surprisingly, the U.S. - have not signed it so far.

In addition to the Universal Declaration of Human Rights, the International Covenant on Civil and Political Rights, the Second Optional Protocol, and the Convention on the Rights of the Child, there are over fifty resolutions adopted by the United Nations General Assembly, the Economic and Social Council, and the United Nations Commission on Human Rights, aimed at total abolition of the death penalty. Many more are in the drafting stage.

In spite of international efforts to abolish the use of the death penalty, capital punishment is still being applied to child offenders, although it is clearly outlawed under the Convention on the Rights of the Child.

Since 1990, eight countries - China, Democratic Republic of Congo, Iran, Nigeria, Pakistan, Saudi Arabia, U.S. and Yemen - have executed 36 child offenders. China, Pakistan, Yemen and Zimbabwe have recently raised the minimum age for the application of the death penalty to 18 years. Iran is in the process of doing the same. However, the Democratic Republic of Congo, Nigeria, Saudi Arabia, and the U.S. still have not outlawed the execution of child offenders.

Since 1990, over half of known executions of child offenders (19 of the 36) have taken place in the U.S. On July 19, 2004, former Presidents Jimmy Carter of the United States and Mikhail Gorbachev of the Russian Federation, along with several other Nobel Peace Prize laureates, lobbied outside the U.S. Supreme Court in Washington D.C. in an effort to end the execution of child offenders.

On March 1, 2005, relying on the "cruel and unusual punishment" provisions of the 8th Amendment, by a narrow margin, the U.S. Supreme Court reversed an earlier ruling and abolished death penalty for juveniles. The Supreme Court cited the overwhelming weight of international opinion as a partial basis for the ruling. In 2006, Iran executed four child offenders and Pakistan one.

United Nations Commission on Human Rights continues with its efforts towards abolishing the death penalty. It appoints Special Rapporteurs on extrajudicial, summary or arbitrary executions to look into independent cases of capital punishment throughout the world and try to prevent new ones, encouraging "the desirability of the abolition of the death penalty" and ensuring that restrictions on its use are upheld.

The United Nations has requested all Member States who are parties to the International Covenant on Civil and Political Rights and have not yet acceded to or ratified the Second Optional Protocol to the International Covenant on Civil and Political Rights, aimed at the abolition of the death penalty, to do so.

The United Nations has been constantly urging all Member States that still maintain the death penalty:

- To comply fully with their obligations under the International Covenant on Civil and Political Rights and the Convention on the Rights of the Child; notably
- Not to impose the death penalty except for the most serious crimes and only pursuant to a final judgement rendered by an independent and impartial competent court;
- Not to impose the death penalty for crimes committed by persons below 18 years of age,
- Not to impose the death penalty on pregnant women;
- Not to impose the death penalty on a person suffering from any form of mental disorder;
- Not to execute any person as long as any related legal procedure, at the international or at the national level, is pending;
- Not to impose the death penalty for non-violent financial crimes;
- Not to impose the death penalty for non-violent religious practice or expression of conscience;
- To ensure the right to a fair trial and the right to seek pardon or commutation of sentence; and
- To ensure that the notion of "most serious crimes" does not go beyond intentional crimes with lethal or extremely grave consequences.

The United Nations has requested all Member States that still maintain the death penalty to:

- Progressively restrict the number of offences for which the death penalty may be imposed;

- To establish a moratorium on executions, with a view to completely abolishing the death penalty;
- To make available to the public information with regard to the imposition of the death penalty

The United Nations has requested all Member States that receive a request for extradition from another country on a capital charge, to reserve explicitly the right to refuse extradition in the absence of effective assurances from relevant authorities of the requesting State that capital punishment will not be carried out.

In June, 2007, the European Union introduced a resolution in the UN General Assembly proposing a world-wide moratorium on executions. On November 1, 2007, the UN General Assembly adopted the resolution calling upon all member states to establish moratorium on the use of the death penalty with a view to abolish the death penalty.

The present stand of the United Nations is a move towards total abolition.

Pretty: My Lordships. I have finished for the day. I thank you all very much.

Justice A: The court is adjourned for the day. We will assemble again tomorrow at 10.30 A.M. sharp.

If I can prove that this punishment is neither useful nor necessary, I will have furthered the cause of humanity.

        Marchese De Cesare Bonesana Beccaria

Day 8

Back to Supreme Court of India's Court Room No. 1. The time is 10.30 A.M. The scene is much the same as yesterday. The judges are in their seats.

Justice A: You may begin.

Pretty: My Lordships. I will tell you about the views of the Council of Europe and the European Union on capital punishment.

During the late 18th century, jurists and reformers started questioning the legitimacy and utility of the death penalty. One of the earliest sustained critics of the death penalty was Marchese De Cesare Bonesana Beccaria.

In 1764, Beccaria published the famous treatise Dei Delitti e della Pen (On Crimes and Punishments) in Italian. The French translation contained anonymous preface by Voltaire. In the preface to this book, first appeared the phrase "the greatest happiness of the greatest number". It advocated the prevention of crime rather than punishment, and promptness in punishment, where punishment was inevitable; above all, it condemned confiscation, capital punishment, and torture.

Beccaria wrote, "If I can prove that this punishment is neither useful nor necessary, I will have furthered the cause of humanity." (Dei delitti e delle pene (1764)).

Moved by compassionate sentiment of a humane feeling, Beccaria asserted that all capital punishment is wrong in itself and unjust. He maintained that since man was not his own creator, he did not have the right to destroy human life, either individually or collectively. It is the ultimate cruel, inhuman and degrading punishment, and violates the right to life.

Beccaria's ideas directly influenced the reforming activities of many social thinkers and philosophers. This represented a school of doctrine, born out of the new humanitarian impulse of the Eighteenth century with which Rousseau, Voltaire and Montesquieu in France and Bentham in England were associated, which came afterwards to be known as the classical school. Montesquieu, Voltaire and other writers wrote against the death penalty.

Beccaria's treatise has been translated into many languages and has become the foundation which many criminology theories have used to build and expand upon. His ideas have influenced the United States' Constitution, Bill of Rights and justice system. The world is still using it to guide criminal justice.

European countries started inching forwards towards abolition of the death penalty. However, early attempts to repeal the death penalty were not always welcome. There were criticisms. There were resistances. There were oppositions. Yet, several countries started restricting the death penalty to capital crimes. The restriction on the use of death penalty to capital crimes continued over the next two centuries.

In spite of opposition and apprehensions, some countries went a step further and abolished the death penalty. Portugal abolished the death penalty in 1867, followed by the Netherlands. Sweden and Denmark joined the abolitionists after the First World War. Italy, Finland and Austria did the same after the Second World War. During the middle of the twentieth century, Germany threw out capital punishment for all crimes. In the 1960s and 1970s, United Kingdom and Spain became abolitionists - for civil crimes.

Pretty: My Lordships. I will tell your Lordships about the views of the Council of Europe, the continent's oldest political organization, which was established in 1949.

The Council of Europe has its headquarters in Strasbourg, in north-eastern France. Its members are 47 countries, including 21 countries from Central and Eastern Europe. It has granted observer status to 5 more countries (the Holy See, the United States, Canada, Japan and Mexico).

It was established under the Statute of the Council of Europe, signed in London on May 5, 1949, by Foreign Affairs Ministers of ten states: Belgium, Denmark, France, Ireland, Italy, Luxembourg, the Netherlands, Norway, Sweden and the United Kingdom.

On November 4, 1950, Members of the Council of Europe signed the Convention for the Protection of Human Rights and Fundamental Freedoms in Rome - the first international legal instrument safeguarding human rights.

On September 18, 1959, the Council of Europe set up the European Court of Human Rights in Strasbourg,

France to deal with the alleged violations of the Convention for the Protection of Human Rights and Fundamental Freedoms of 1950.

The Parliamentary Assembly of the Council of Europe has all along taken the issue of abolition of the death penalty as one of its major objectives and gradually persuaded member states to abandon the death penalty so that Europe might become the first death penalty free region in the world.

The persistent endeavours of the Council of Europe culminated in success with the adoption of Protocol No 6 to the European Human Rights Convention in Strasbourg on April 28, 1983. The Protocol became effective from March 1, 1985. From this date, the Protocol abolished the death penalty for all civil crimes. And every country seeking membership of the Council of Europe had to agree to ratify Protocol No 6 and to introduce an immediate moratorium on executions. A number of mechanisms were set up to monitor these commitments while assisting governments and parliaments with their implementation.

Article 1 of this Protocol which reads "The death penalty shall be abolished. No-one shall be condemned to such penalty or executed" effectively abolished the death penalty for all civil crimes. Article 2 which reads "A State may make provision in its law for the death penalty in respect of acts committed in time of war or of imminent threat of war; but such penalty shall be applied only in the instances laid down in the law and in accordance with its provisions" allowed retention of the death penalty for war crimes. But the Protocol did not permit any other derogation or reservation from these provisions.

On November 1, 1998, Members of the Council of Europe signed Protocol No. 11 to the Council's European Convention on Human Rights establishing a single permanent European Court of Human Rights in Strasbourg, replacing the old part time European Court.

On May 3, 2002, Members of the Council of Europe signed Protocol 13 to the European Convention on Human Rights, abolishing the death penalty in all circumstances.

However, all the Members of the Council of Europe have not accepted the Protocol so far. In other words, all member countries have not abolished the death penalty.

Pretty: My Lordships. I will now tell you about the views of the European Union. The European Union is often confused with the Council of Europe. The 27-nation European Union is different from the Council of Europe. But no country has ever joined the European Union without first belonging to the Council of Europe.

The first steps towards formation of the present European Union (EU) (formerly known as European Community (EC) or European Economic Community (EEC)) began in the 1950s.

In 1950, the French Foreign Minister, Robert Schuman proposed integrating the coal and steel industries of Western Europe. As a result, in 1951, six member countries - Belgium, West Germany, Luxembourg, France, Italy and the Netherlands set up the European Coal and Steel Community (ECSC). The ECSC gave the power to take decisions relating to the coal and steel industry in the six member countries to an independent, supranational body called the "High Authority".

The ECSC was a great success. The six member countries decided to integrate other sectors of their economies. On March 25, 1957, they signed the Treaties of Rome, creating the European Atomic Energy Community (EURATOM) and the European Economic Community (EEC). The six member countries set about removing trade barriers between themselves and creating a "common market".

In 1967, the three institutions of the European Community - European Coal and Steel Community, European Atomic Energy Community and European Economic Community were merged. Under the new scheme, there was a single Commission and a single Council of Ministers as well as the European Parliament. The Treaty of Maastricht of 1992 introduced new forms of co-operation between the member state governments and created the European Union (EU) from November 1, 1993.

Over the years, the European Union has grown in size and consists of the following 27 members states:

- Austria (1995) (EUR)
- Belgium (founding member: 1952/58) (EUR)
- Bulgaria (2007)
- Cyprus (2004)
- Czech Republic (2004)

- Denmark (1973)
- Estonia (2004)
- Finland (1995) (EUR)
- France (founding member: 1952/58) (EUR)
- Germany (founding member: 1952/58) (EUR)
- Greece (1981) (EUR)
- Hungary (2004)
- Ireland (1973) (EUR)
- Italy (founding member: 1952/58) (EUR)
- Latvia (2004)
- Lithuania (2004)
- Luxembourg (founding member: 1952/58) (EUR)
- Malta (2004)
- The Netherlands (founding member: 1952/58) (EUR)
- Poland (2004) (EUR)
- Portugal (1986)
- Romania (2007)
- Slovakia (2004)
- Slovenia (2004) (EUR)
- Spain (1986) (EUR)
- Sweden (1995)
- United Kingdom (1973)

Note:*EUR denotes countries which have adopted Euro currency.*

Some more countries - Croatia, Norway, Republic of Macedonia, Switzerland, Turkey and Ukraine, are at various stages of negotiations and expected to join the European Union in the coming years.

The European Union may soon expand to over 30 countries. The co-operation of so many countries, who had remained divided for so many years, spells good for the future; but also places heavy demands on all the countries involved.

In December 2000, members of the European Union entered into the Treaty of Nice (at Nice). This new treaty is intended to create a new Constitution for the European Union governing the size of the European Union institutions and the way they would work in future. Its main aims are to replace the overlapping set of existing treaties that comprise the European Union's current constitution, and to streamline decision-making in what is now a 27-member organisation.

The constitutional treaty was signed by representatives of the member states, and has since been ratified by all the member states. The European Commission acts through a cabinet of 27 commissioners (one from each state) headed by the President.

The present cabinet is the Barroso Commission named after its president José Manuel Barroso, who presides over 26 other commissioners (one from each state). The Barroso Commission has been in office since November 22, 2004. Its term expires on October 31, 2009.

Despite its name, the European Union does not cover all countries of Europe in the geographical sense.

Pretty: My Lordships. When the Council of Europe was formed in 1949, all the founder states had the death penalty in their laws, although some countries did not carry out the sentence in practice.

Gradually, the Council of Europe strived towards abolition of the death penalty.

The European Parliament is the parliamentary body of the European Union. The European Parliament had declared that it "considers capital punishment an inhuman, medieval form of punishment and unworthy of modern societies". The European Union strived forward to abolish the death penalty for all crimes, including crimes under military law or those committed in exceptional circumstances - such as during wartime.

In 1998, the Member States of the European Union decided to strengthen their activities in opposition to the death penalty and they adopted guidelines to this end. By this time, capital punishment had been abolished in most of the Member States of the European Union and those that had not yet abolished it were not applying it. Since then, all states of the Union have ratified Protocol No 6 to the European Convention on Human Rights concerning the Abolition of the Death Penalty. It should also be noted that abolition forms one of the conditions of membership to the European Union.

The European Union not only made its members adopt total abolition, it has been requesting other countries to do the same. For several years, within the framework of the United Nations, the European Union has requested countries where the death penalty still exists to gradually restrict the number of crimes punishable by death and to establish a moratorium on executions. The objective is to attain complete abolition of the death penalty.

Furthermore, the European Union is working in collaboration with non-governmental organisations (NGOs), in particular through the European Initiative for Democracy and Human Rights (EIDHR), towards the universal abolition of the death penalty.

Pretty: My Lordships. A private organization, Ensemble contre la peine de mortonm (Together against the Death Penalty) organised the First World Congress against the Death Penalty in Strasbourg on 21, 22 and 23 June 2001. It issued the following declaration:

"We, citizens and abolitionist campaigners gathered in Strasbourg from 21 to 23 June 2001 for the First World Congress against the Death Penalty, organised by Ensemble contre la peine de mort, declare:

The death penalty means the triumph of vengeance over justice and violates the first right of any human being, the right to life. Capital punishment has never prevented crime. It is an act of torture and the ultimate cruel, inhuman and degrading treatment. A society that imposes the death penalty symbolically encourages violence. Every single society that respects the dignity of its people has to strive to abolish capital punishment.

We are pleased to note that many Speakers of Parliament have decided to launch on 22 June a "Solemn appeal for a world-wide moratorium on executions of those sentenced to death as a step towards universal abolition" at the European Parliament. We demand the universal abolition of the death penalty. In this respect, we call on citizens, states and international organizations to act so that:

▶ states ratify all abolitionist treaties and conventions on an international and regional level.

▶ countries which have stopped executing people sentenced to death, remove the death penalty from their statute books.

▶ states which sentence to death persons who were juveniles at the time of the crime, end this blatant violation of the international law.

▶ mentally disabled people cannot be sentenced to death.

▶ no states having abolished or suspended executions extradite anyone to third countries still applying the death penalty, irrespective of guarantees that it would not be imposed.

▶ states regularly and openly publish information on death sentences, detention conditions and executions.

We support the investigation of the Council of Europe on the compatibility of the observer status of the United States and Japan with their adherence of the death penalty.

We call on the Council of Europe and the European Union to insist that Turkey, Russia and Armenia permanently abolish the death penalty for ALL crimes and commute all death sentences.

We call on the European Union to continue its efforts to achieve the abolition of the death penalty and thus, in the ordinary course of its international relations.

In addition to these general recommendations, we will issue specific recommendations, on a country-by-country basis, to support abolitionist campaigners.

We commit ourselves to creating a world-wide co-ordination of associations and abolitionist campaigners, whose first goal will be to launch a world-wide day for the universal abolition of the death penalty.

We call on the judicial and medical professions to confirm the utter incompatibility of their values with the death penalty and to intensify, country-by-country, their activities against the death penalty.

We associate ourselves with the petitions collected by Amnesty International, the Community of Sant' Egidio, Ensemble contre la peine de mort, the Federation of Human Rights League, Hands off Cain and any other organizations and call on all abolitionist campaigners to sign the following international petition :

"We, citizens of the world, call for an immediate halt of all executions of those sentenced to death and the universal abolition of the death penalty"

Lastly, we call upon every state to take all possible steps towards the adoption by the United Nations of a world-wide moratorium on executions, pending universal abolition.

Strasbourg, 22 June 2001."

Pretty: My Lordships. Ensemble contre la peine de mort (Together against the Death Penalty), Penal Reform International in collaboration with Amnesty International-Canada and other Canadian groups, organised the Second World Congress against the Death Penalty in Montreal from 6 to 8 October 2004.

The Congress heard testimonies from relatives of murder victims and former death row prisoners. They heard statements by UN officials, governmental representatives, members of various professions and celebrities.

In a final declaration, the Congress reaffirmed that executions fail to address the pain and suffering of victims of crime. The Congress welcomed the fact that "more and more victims' families are now working against the death penalty" and called on all countries "to develop appropriate mechanisms to address their needs".

Pretty: My Lordships. Ensemble contre la peine de mort (Together against the Death Penalty) and the World Coalition against the Death Penalty organized the Third World Congress against the Death Penalty in Paris from February 1-3, 2007. The Congress once again called upon all countries to abolish the capital punishment and to stop executions. The World Congress also called upon abolitionists all over the world, all regional and international organisations and the European Union to adopt 10 October as the World Day against the Death Penalty.

Pretty: My Lordships. In the majority of European States, total abolition of capital punishment was achieved in two stages - of which the second was, in general, a lengthy process.

Some countries, such as, United Kingdom, Spain, Luxembourg, France, Ireland, Greece and Belgium retained the death penalty in their laws till the second half of the last century. But executions took place very rarely or the death penalty simply remained unused.

In fact, in most countries there was a long period of time between the carrying out of the last execution and actual abolition of the death penalty, which indicates that European countries had already become abolitionist de facto, or even by tradition, long before they formally abandoned capital punishment. In these countries, the capital punishment had clearly fallen into disuse in actual practice.

On the other hand, while in some EU Member States abolitionist measures have met the deep sentiment of the population and thus corresponded to the accomplishment of a national tradition, in others the political decision towards abolition was not taken with the support of the majority of public opinion.

Nevertheless in countries where this was the case, the decision did not result in any form of negative reaction, usually leading to minimal debate on the issue. Therefore, mention should be made of the fact that abolition itself contributed favourably to better-informed public opinion, which helped to shape different feelings among community members.

The present position of the European Union is that:

- All the Member States of the EU have abandoned the capital punishment for all crimes.
- Abolition is a requirement for countries seeking EU membership.
- Almost all the candidate countries have acceded to Protocol No. 6 to the European Convention on Human Rights concerning the Abolition of the Death Penalty. There is only one exception: Turkey.
- The EU believes no matter how cruel the crime committed by the offender may be, the death penalty is inhuman, unnecessary and irreversible.
- The EU is opposed to the death penalty in all circumstances and has agreed to campaign for its universal abolition.
- The EU believes that it is impossible to reduce to zero the risk of applying the penalty in error. That risk alone, the risk of taking an innocent life, is enough reason to outlaw it as a punishment.
- The EU does not accept the argument that the death penalty is a deterrent to violent crime. The EU believes that the evidence in their countries simply does not support this claim.
- The EU is working towards the universal abolition of the death penalty.
- Where the death penalty still exists, the EU calls for its use to be progressively restricted, and insists that it be carried out according to minimum standards.

- The EU also actively pursues this policy in international human rights fora. An example of this is the EU call for moving a resolution in the forthcoming UN General Assembly calling for a universal moratorium on the death penalty.
- The EU introduced the text, which calls on states to consider acceding to the Second Optional Protocol to the International Covenant on Civil and Political Rights. This instrument is aimed at abolishing the death penalty and to ensure that - in states where death penalty has not yet been eradicated it is only imposed for the most serious crimes and to establish a moratorium on executions. The resolution, amassing more than 60 co-sponsors, was adopted after a roll-call vote: of 53 CHR Members, 27 voted for, 18 against and 7 abstained.
- The EU is promoting and assisting programmes for promotion of human rights and democracy through mobilisation of public opinion against capital punishment.

Where states insist on maintaining the death penalty, the EU considers it important that the following minimum standards should be met:

- Capital punishment may be imposed only for the most serious crimes, it being understood that their scope should not go beyond intentional crimes with lethal or other extremely grave consequences. The death penalty should not be imposed for non-violent financial crimes or for non-violent religious practice or expression of conscience.
- Capital punishment may be imposed only for a crime for which the death penalty was

prescribed at the time of its commission, it being understood that if, subsequent to the commission of the crime, provision is made by law for the imposition of a lighter penalty, the offender shall benefit thereby.
- Capital punishment may not be imposed on: Persons below 18 years of age at the time of the commission of their crime;
- Pregnant women or new mothers;
- Persons who have become insane.
- Capital punishment may be imposed only when the guilt of the person charged is based upon clear and convincing evidence leaving no room for alternative explanation of the facts.
- Capital punishment must only be carried out pursuant to a final judgement rendered by a competent court after legal process which gives all possible safeguards to ensure a fair trial, at least equal to those contained in Article 14 of the International Covenant on Civil and Political Rights, including the right of anyone suspected of or charged with a crime for which capital punishment may be imposed to adequate legal assistance at all stages of the proceedings, and where appropriate, the right to contact a consular representative.
- Anyone sentenced to death shall have an effective right to appeal to a court of higher jurisdiction, and steps should be taken to ensure that such appeals become mandatory.
- Where applicable, anyone sentenced to death shall have the right to submit an individual complaint under international procedures; the death sentence will not be carried out while

the complaint remains under consideration under those procedures.
- Anyone sentenced to death shall have the right to seek pardon or commutation of the sentence. Amnesty, pardon or commutation of the sentence of death may be granted in all cases of capital punishment.
- Capital punishment may not be carried out in contravention of a state's international commitments.
- The length of time spent after having been sentenced to death may also be a factor.
- Where capital punishment occurs, it shall be carried out so as to inflict the minimum possible suffering. It may not be carried out in public or in any other degrading manner.
- The death penalty should not be imposed as an act of political revenge in contravention of the minimum standards, e.g. against coup plotters.

As a group, the European Union is the strongest force within the United Nations which has abolished the death penalty for all offences - civil as well as military and is now aggressively trying to extend the prohibition on the death penalty to countries like Japan and the U.S.

In June, 2007, the European Union introduced a resolution in the UN General Assembly proposing a world-wide moratorium on executions. On November 1, 2007, the UN General Assembly adopted the resolution calling upon all member states to establish moratorium on the use of the death penalty with a view to abolish the death penalty.

Pretty: My Lordships. I have finished for the day. I thank you all very much.

Justice A: The court is adjourned for the day. We will assemble again tomorrow at 10.30 A.M. sharp.

But where life and death are at stake, inconsistencies which are understandable may not be acceptable.

Prof. Blackshield

Day 9

Back to Supreme Court of India's Court Room No. 1. The time is 10.30 A.M. The scene is much the same as in the previous days. The judges are in their seats.

Justice A: You may begin.

Pretty: My Lordships. I will now discuss the law in India. Earlier, the alternative sentences of death or imprisonment for life provided for murder and for certain other capital offences under the Indian Penal Code, were the normal sentences.

Section 354 (3) of the Code of Criminal Procedure 1898, marks a significant shift in the legislative policy underlying the Code from April 1, 1974.

Now, according to this changed legislative policy which is patent onthe face of section 354 (3), the *normal* punishment for murder and six other capital offences under the Penal Code is imprisonment for life (or imprisonment for a term of years) and the death penalty is an exception.

I will now take you through some decisions of this Honourable Court on the constitutional validity of the death penalty.

The Supreme Court first considered the constitutional validity of the death penalty in Bachan Singh vs. State of Punjab (1983) 1 SCR 145. By a majority decision, the Supreme Court held that the provision of death penalty, as an alternative punishment for murder, was constitutionally valid and did not violate either the letter or the ethos of Article 19. However, in this decision, Bhagwati, J. (as he then was), gave a dissenting judgment. He held that the death penalty was bad morally as well as constitutionally. (Bhagwati, J. has continued to oppose the death penalty to this day.)

The Supreme Court examined this aspect in several cases. In Smt. Triveniben vs. State of Gujarat, (1989) 1 SCC 678, a Constitution Bench of five learned Judges - comprising Justices G. L. Oza, M. M. Dutt, K. N. Singh, K. Jagannatha Shetty and L. M. Sharma considered this question once again. They delivered two concurring judgments on February 7, 1989. One by Justice Jagannatha Shetty on behalf of himself; and the other majority judgement by Justice G. L. Oza on behalf of himself and the remaining three judges. They agreed with the decision in Bachan Singh's case and upheld the constitutional validity of the death penalty.

Pretty: My Lordships. I will now take you through some more decisions of this Hon'ble Court on the death penalty. The first case I will take you through is the case of Dhananjoy Chatterjee vs. State of W. B. which was decided in 1994.

A young 18 year old school-going girl, Hetal Parekh, was raped and murdered on March 5, 1990 between 5.30 and 5.45p.m. in her Flat No. 3-A, on the third floor of 'Anand Apartment' in Kolkatta. Dhananjoy Chatterjee, who was a security guard of the building, was arrested and tried for murder, rape and also for committing theft of a wrist-watch from the said flat.

The Additional Sessions Judge found Dhananjoy Chatterjee guilty of all three crimes and convicted him:

(i) for the offence under Section 302 IPC and sentenced him to death,
(ii) for the offence under Section 376 IPC and sentenced him to imprisonment for life, and
(iii) for the offence under Section 380 IPC, he was sentenced to undergo rigorous imprisonment for five years.

The sentences under Sections 376 and 380 IPC were to run concurrently but were to cease to have any effect, in case the sentence of death for conviction of Dhananjoy Chatterjee under Section 302 IPC was confirmed by the High Court and he was executed. Since a sentence of death has to be necessarily referred to the High Court, the Additional Sessions Judge referred the death sentence to the High Court of Calcutta for confirmation.

Dhananjoy Chatterjee preferred an appeal against his conviction and sentence in the High Court. The High Court dismissed the appeal filed by Dhananjoy Chatterjee and confirmed the sentence of death. Dhananjoy Chatterjee filed appeal before the Supreme Court.

The Supreme Court held: "We are therefore in complete agreement with the trial court and the High Court that the prosecution has established the guilt of the appellant beyond a reasonable doubt and we, therefore, uphold his conviction for the offences under Sections 302, 376 and 380 IPC.

"This now brings us to the question of sentence. The trial court awarded the sentence of death and the High Court confirmed the imposition of capital punishment for the offence under Section 302 IPC for the murder of Hetal Parekh. Learned counsel submitted that appellant was a married man of 27 years of age and there were no special reasons to award the sentence of death on him. Learned counsel submitted that keeping in view the legislative policy discernible from Section 235(2) read with Section 354(3) CrPC, the Court may make the choice of not imposing the extreme penalty of death on the appellant and give him a chance to become a reformed member of the society in keeping with the concern for the dignity of human life. Learned counsel for the State has on the other hand canvassed for confirmation of the sentence of death so that it serves as a deterrent to similar depraved minds. According to the learned State counsel there were no mitigating circumstances and the case was undoubtedly "rarest of the rare" cases where the sentence of death alone would meet the ends of justice.

"We have given our anxious consideration to the question of sentence keeping in view the changed legislative policy which is patent from Section 354(3) CrPC. We have also considered the observations of this Court in Bachan Singh case.

"In recent years, the rising crime rate particularly violent crime against women has made the criminal sentencing by the courts a subject of concern. Today there are admitted disparities. Some criminals get very harsh sentences while many receive grossly different sentence for an essentially equivalent crime and a shockingly large number even go unpunished thereby encouraging the criminal and in the ultimate making justice suffer by weakening the system's credibility. Of course, it is not possible to lay down any cut and dry formula relating to imposition of sentence but the object of sentencing should be to see that the crime does not go unpunished and the victim of crime as also the society has the satisfaction that justice has been done to it. In imposing sentences in the absence of specific legislation, Judges must consider variety of factors and after considering all those factors and taking an overall view of the situation, impose sentence which they consider to be an appropriate one. Aggravating factors cannot be ignored and similarly mitigating circumstances have also to be taken into consideration.

"In our opinion, the measure of punishment in a given case must depend upon the atrocity of the crime; the conduct of the criminal and the defenceless and unprotected state of the victim. Imposition of appropriate punishment is the manner in which the courts respond to the society's cry for justice against the criminals. Justice demands that courts should impose punishment befitting the crime so that the courts reflect public abhorrence of the crime. The courts must not only keep in view the rights of the criminal but also the rights of the victim of crime and the society at large while considering imposition of appropriate punishment.

"The sordid episode of the security guard, whose sacred duty was to ensure the protection and welfare of the inhabitants of the flats in theapartment, shoulhave subjected the deceased, a resident of one of the flats,to gratify his lust and murder her in retaliation for his transfer on her complaint, makes the crime even more heinous. Keeping in view the medical evidence and the state in which the body of the deceased was found, it is obvious that a most heinous type of barbaric rape and murder was committed on a helpless and defenceless school-going girl of 18 years. If the security guards behave in this manner who will guard the guards? The faith of the society by such a barbaric act of the guard, gets totally shaken and its cry for justice becomes loud and clear. The offence was not only inhuman and barbaric but it was a totally ruthless crime of rape followed by cold blooded murder and an affront to the human dignity of the society. The savage nature of the crime has shocked our judicial conscience. There are no extenuating or mitigating circumstances whatsoever in the case. We agree that a real and abiding concern for the dignity of human life is required to be kept in mind by the courts while considering the confirmation of the sentence of death but a cold blooded preplanned brutal murder, without any provocation, after committing rape on an innocent and defenceless young girl of 18 years, by the security guard certainly makes this case a "rarest of the rare" cases which calls for no punishment other than the capital punishment and we accordingly confirm the sentence of death imposed upon the appellant for the offence under Section 302 IPC."

Dhananjoy Chatterjee Vs. State of W. B.
Citation: 1994 SCR (1) 37; 1994 SCC (2) 220
Date of Judgement 11.01.1994
Judgment was delivered by Dr. Anand, A.S. (J)
The Supreme Court bench consisted of Anand, A.S. (J) and Singh, N.P. (J)

Pretty: My Lordships. I will now take you through the decision of this Honorable Court in the case of State of Uttar Pradesh vs. Devendra Singh. This decision was rendered in 2004.

On 26.12.1978, at about noon, the deceased girl, aged about 10 years, went to the 'Kolhu' of Rajendra Singh, father of Devendra Singh, the accused, in order to chew sugarcane. She was seen chewing sugarcane at the 'Kolhu'. She did not return home.

Next day, some persons went to the sugarcane field to search for the deceased girl. Devendra Singh did not allow them to look inside the sugarcane field. Thereafter, they brought the pradhan (village chief) and some other persons of the village and searched for the deceased in the sugarcane field.

During the search, some portion of the field towards the south was found to be freshly dug. This place was dug. The dead body of the deceased was found buried there.

Devendra Singh was tried for the rape and murder of the deceased girl. The Trial Court found Devendra Singh guilty and sentenced him to imprisonment for life. In appeal, a Division Bench of the Allahabad High Court reversed the judgment of the Trial Court and directed acquittal.

The State of Uttar Pradesh appealed to the Supreme Court questioning the legality of the judgment rendered by the Division Bench of the Allahabad High Court in setting aside the conviction of Devendra Singh.

The Supreme Court found that the dead body was found in the field of Devendra Singh; that initially he had prevented the persons from searching his field; only after lot of persuasions he permitted the persons searching for the dead body to enter his field; and in fact the dead body was recovered from there.

The Supreme Court held that the circumstances, coupled with the initial repulsion exhibited by Devendra Singh, substantiated his guilt. They held that the evidence on record led to the inevitable conclusion that Devendra Singh was responsible for the rape and murder of the victim.

The Supreme Court held that "in view of the patently perverse conclusions arrived at by the High Court, the same is indefensible and is set aside. The conviction as recorded by the Trial Court and the sentences imposed are restored. Accused shall surrender to custody forthwith to serve the sentence imposed by the Trial Court."

My lords, in this case too, there was the unfortunate rape and murder of a ten year old girl. But the Supreme Court only confirmed the sentence awarded by the Trial Court - imprisonment for life.

State of Uttar Pradesh Vs. Devendra Singh
Case No.: Appeal (crl.) 617 of 1998
Date of judgement 13.4.2004
Judgement was delivered by Arijit Pasayat(J).
The Supreme Court bench consisted of Doraiswamy Raju (J) and Arijit Pasayat (J).

Pretty: My Lordships. I will now take you through the consolidated decision of this Honorable

Court in three separate appeals. The majority (2:1) judgement was delivered in 1979 Justice V. R. Krishna Iyer one of the greatest Judges of all time.

The first case is Rajendra Prasad's case. In the words of Justice Krishna Iyer "a long-standing family feud, with years-long roots, led to a tragic murder. The houses of Ram Bharosey and Pyarelal had fallen out and periodic fuelling of the feud was furnished by the kidnapping of a wife, the stabbing of a brother and the like. Lok Adalats of village elders brought about truce, not peace. The next flare-up was a murder by the appellant, a rash son of one of the feuding elders Pyarelal. He was sentenced to life imprisonment (which means no reformation but hardening process, since our jails are innocent of carefully designed programme of re-humanizing but have an iatrogenic, inherited drill of de-humanising).

"The young man, after some years served in prison, was released on Gandhi Jayanti Day. But Gandhian hospital setting was, perhaps, absent in the prison which, in all probability, was untouched by reformation of diseased minds, the fundamental Gandhian thought. The result was the release kept alive his vendetta on return, aggravated by the 'zoological' life inside. Some minor incident ignited his latent feud and he stabbed Ram Bharosey and his friend Mansukh several times, and the latter succumbed. The 'desperate character' once sentenced, deserved death this second time, said the Sessions Court and the High Court confirmed the view.

"An application of the canons we have laid down directly arises. There is the common confusion here.

A second murder is not to be confounded with the persistent potential for murderous attacks by the murderer. This was not a menace to the social order but a specific family feud. While every crime is a breach of social peace, the assailant is bound over only if he is a public menace. Likewise, here was not a youth of uncontrollable violent propensities against the community but one whose paranoid preoccupation with a family quarrel goaded him to go at the rival. The distinction is fine but real. How do we designate him 'desperate' without blaming the jail which did little to make a man out of the criminal clay? So long as therapeutic processes are absent from prisons, these institutions, far from being the healing hope of society, prove hardening schools to train desperate criminals. The pitiless verse of Oscar Wilde is pitifully true even today:

> "The vilest deeds, like poison weeds,
> Bloom well in prison air;
> It is only what is good in Man
> That wastes and withers there"

'Desperate criminal' is a convenient description to brand a person. Seldom is the other side of the story exposed to judicial view - the failure of penal institutions to cure criminality and their success in breaking the spirit or embittering it.

"Prasad's prison term never 'cured' him. Who bothered about cure? The blame for the second murder is partly on this neglect. Nothing on record suggests that Rajendra Prasad was beyond redemption; nothing on record hints at any such attempt inside the prison Lock-up of a criminal for long years behind stone walls and iron bars, with drills of breaking themorale, willnot change the prisoner for the better. Recidivism is an index of prison failure, in most cases. Any way, Rajendra showed no incurable disposition to violent outbursts against his fellow-men. We see no special reason, to hang him out of corporeal existence. But while awarding him life imprisonment instead, we direct for him mental-moral healing courses through suitable work, acceptable meditational techniques and psycho-therapic drills to regain his humanity and dignity. Prisons are not human warehouses but humane retrieval homes.

"Even going by precedents like Lalla Singh (supra) this convict has had the hanging agony hanging over his head since 1973, with near solitary confinement to boot. He must, by now, be more a vegetable than a person and hanging a vegetable is not death penalty. This is an additional ground for our reduction."

The second case is the Kunjukunju Janardanan case. In the words of Justice Krishna Iyer, this case "is no different in the result but very different on the facts. The scenario is the usual sex triangle, terribly perverted. One randy Janardanan - the appellant - with a wife and two children, developed sex relations with a fresh girl and the inevitable social resistance to this betrayal of marital fidelity led to a barbaric short-cut by this criminal of cutting to death the innocent wife and the immaculate kids in the secrecy of night. To borrow the vivid words of the courts below, 'deliberate', 'cold-blooded' was the act, attended as it was with 'considerable brutality'. This ruled out mitigation and supplied 'special reasons', according to both the courts below, for the awesome award of death penalty. Was that right? If the crime alone was the criterion, yes; but if the criminal was the target, no.

"The crucial question is whether the crime and its horrendous character except to the extent it reveals irreparable depravity and chronic propensity is relevant. The innocent three will not be happy because one guilty companion is also added to their number. Is Janardanan a social security risk, altogether beyond salvage by therapeutic life sentence? If he is, the pall must fall on his cadaver. If not, life must burn on. So viewed, no material, save juridical wrath and grief, is discernible to invoke social justice and revoke his fundamental right to life. A course of anti-aphrodisiac treatment or willing castration is a better recipe for this hypersexed human than outright death sentence. We have not even information on whether he was a desperate hedonist or any rapist with 'Y' chromosomes in excess, who sipped every flower and changed every hour, so as to be a sex menace to the locality. Sentencing is a delicate process, not a blind man's buff. We commute the death sentence to life imprisonment."

The third case is the Dubey case. In the words of Justice Krishna Iyer again, in this case "There were three accused to begin with. The appellant was convicted of the murder of three relatives and sentenced to death. The other two were held guilty, by the Sessions Judge of an offence ofs.302 read with s. 34 I.P.C. and awarded life imprisonment. The appeal of the latter was allowed and that of the former dismissed both on crime and punishment.

"The learned Judges expressed themselves thus: 'Considering that Sheo Shankar, appellant caused the death of three persons so closely related to him, by stabbing each of them in the chest one after the other, and that too on no greater provocation than that there had been an exchange of abuses, I do not see how it can be said that sentence of death errs on the side of severity. It was urged that this appellant was only 17, 18 years old and so in view of the ruling of the Supreme Court in Harnam v. State (AIR 1976 SC 2071), he should not be sentenced to death. In the first place, the note of learned Sessions Judge on his statement shows that he was 19, 20 years old and he had understated his age. Secondly, I doubt that the observation of the Supreme Court in the said case can be applicable to such a case of triple murder, where such victim is deliberately stabbed in the chest.'

"The whole reasoning crumbles on a gentle probe. A thumbnail sketch of the case is that the appellant, his father and his brother were angrily dissatisfied with a family partition and, on the tragic day, flung the vessels over the division of which the wrangle arose, went inside the house, emerged armed, picked up an altercation eventuating in the young man (whose age was around 18 or 20) stabbing to death three members of the other branch of the family. He chased and killed, excited by the perverted sense of injustice at the partition. It is illegal to award capital sentence without considering the correctional possibilities inside prison. Anger, even judicial anger, solves no problems but creates many.

"Have the courts below regarded the question of sentence from this angle? Not at all. The genesis of the crime shows a family feud. He was not a murderer born but made by the passion of family quarrel. He could be saved for society with correctional techniques and directed into repentance like the Chambal dacoits.

"What startles us is the way the adolescence of the accused has been by-passed and a ruling of this Court reduced to a casualty by a casual observation. Hardly the way decisions of the Supreme Court, read with Art. 141 should be by-passed.

"Had the appellant been only 18 years of age, he would not have been sentenced to death as the High Court expressly states. The High Court is right in stating so. Tender age is a tender circumstance and in this country, unlike in England of old, children are not executed. Since the age of the accused is of such critical importance in a marginal situation like the present one, one should have expected from the courts below a closer examination of that aspect.

"Unfortunately, they have not got the accused medically examined for his age nor have they received any specific evidence on the point but have disposed of the question in a rather summary way: 'In the first place, the note of the learned Sessions Judge on his statement shows that he was 19/20 years old and he had understated his age. Secondly, I doubt that the observations of the Supreme Court in the said case (AIR 1976 SC 2071) can be applicable to such a case of triple murder, where each victim is deliberately stabbed in the chest.' A judge is no expert in fixing the age of a person and when precise age becomes acutely important reliance on medical and other testimony is necessary. One cannot agree with this manner of disposal of a vital factor bearing on so grave an issue as death sentence. Nor are we satisfied with the court vaguely distinguishing a ruling of this Court. It is not the number of deaths caused nor the situs of the stabs that is telling on that decision to validate the non-application of its ratio. It is a mechanistic art which counts the cadavers to sharpen the sentence oblivious of other crucial criteria shaping a dynamic, realistic policy of punishment.

"Three deaths are regrettable, indeed, terrible. But it is no social solution to add one more life lost to the list. In this view, we are satisfied that the appellant has not received reasonable consideration on the question of the appropriate sentence. The criteria we have laid down are clear enough to point to the softening of the sentence to one of life imprisonment. A family feud, an altercation, a sudden passion, although attended with extra-ordinary cruelty, young and malleable age, reasonable prospect of reformation and absence of any conclusive circumstance that the assailantis a habitual murderer or given to chronic violence - these catena of circumstancesbearingon the offender call for the lesser sentence.

"It is apt to notice in this context that even on a traditional approach this is not a case for death sentence, if we are to be belighted by the guidelines in Carlose John. The murder there was brutal but the act was committed while the accused were in a grip of emotional stress. This was regarded as persuasive enough, in the background of the case, to avoid the extreme penalty. The ruling in Kartar Singh related to a case of brutal murder and of hired murderers with planning of the criminal project. In that background, the affirmation of the death sentence, without any discussion of the guidelines as between 'life' and 'death' awards was hardly meant as a mechanical formula. It is difficult to discern any such ratio in that ruling on the question of sentence in the grey area of life versus death. The holding was surely right even by the tests we have indicated but to decoct a principle that if three lives are taken, death sentence is the sequel, is to read, without warrant, into that decision a reversal of the process spread over decades.

"Social defence against murderers is best insured in the short run by caging them but in the long run, the real run, by transformation through re-orientation of the inner man by many methods including neuro-techniques of which we have a rich legacy.If the prison system will talk the native language, we have the yogic treasure to experiment with on high- strung, high-risk murder merchants. Neuroscience stands on the threshold of astounding discoveries. Yoga, in its many forms, seems to hold splendid answers. Meditational technology as a tool of criminology is a mascent-ancient methodology. The State must experiment. It is cheaper to hang than to heal, but Indian life - any human life - is too dear to be swung dead save in extreme circumstances.

"We are painfully mindful that this Judgment has become prolix and diffuse. But too many pages are not too high a price where death sentence jurisprudence demands de novo examination to do justice by the Constitution.

"Much of what we have said is an exercise in penal philosophy in the critical area of death sentence.

"Philosophizing is distrusted by most of the professions that are concerned with the penal system. It is suspect for lawyers because they are conscious that if the criminal law as a whole is the Cinderella of jurisprudence, then the law of sentencing is Cinderella's illegitimate baby."

"After all, the famous words of Justice Holmes 'The Law must keep its promises' must be remembered.

"The appeals stand allowed and the death sentences stand reduced to life imprisonment; and, hopefully, human rights stand vindicated."

CRIMINAL APPELLATE JURISDICTION:

Criminal Appeal No. 512 of 1978. Appeal by Special Leave from the Judgment and Order dated 12-9-74 of the Allahabad High Court in Criminal Appeal No. 501/74.

AND

Criminal Appeal No. 513 of 1978. Appeal by Special Leave from the Judgment and Order dated 9-1-1978 of the Kerala High Court in Criminal Appeal No. 213/77 and Ref. Trial No. 3/77.

AND

Criminal Appeal. 513 of 1978
Appeal by Special Leave from the Judgment and Order
dated 28-9-77 of the Allahabad High Court in Criminal Appeal
No. 261/73 and Reference No. 6/77.

Citation:1979 AIR916;1979 SCR (3) 78;1979 SCC(3) 646
Date of judgement9.02.1979
Judgement was delivered by Krishna Aiyer, V. R.(J). The Supreme Court bench consisted of Krishna Aiyer, V. R.(J), Desai, D.A. (J) and Sen, A. P. (J).

Pretty: My Lordships. The Lalla Singh's case involved murder of three persons. The head of one of the deceased, a lady, was severed. The trial judge awarded the extreme penalty of death to the murderer.

But the court reduced the sentence to life imprisonment on the ground of the long and agonising gap between the date of offence and the disposal of the case by the Supreme Court. The Supreme Court observed "While we are unable to say that the learned Sessions Judge was in error in imposing the extreme penalty, we feel that as the offence was committed on 18-6-1971 more than six years ago, the ends of justice do not require that we should confirm the sentence of death passed on the first respondent."

My Lordships. These few decisions show that even the Supreme Court has not been consistent. One can not really understand why one convict is sent to the gallows, while another convict almost in identical circumstances, is given the lesser sentence of imprisonment for life. I have finished for the day.

Justice A: The court is adjourned for the day. We will assemble again tomorrow at 10.30 A.M. sharp.

Several attempts have been made to restrict or remove death penaltyunder Section 302 butnever even once to enlarge its application.

Parliamentary pressure has been to cut down death penalty, although the section formally remains the same and is very nearly being wholly recast benignly.

The cue for the Court is clear.

Justice V. R. Krishna Aiyer

Law does not stand still. It moves continually. Once this is recognised, then the task of the Judge is put on a higher plane. He must consciously seek to mould the law so as to serve the needs of the time.

He must not be a mere mechanic, a mere working mason, laying brick on brick, without thought to the overall design. He must be an architect - thinking of the structure as a whole, building for society a system of law which is strong, durable and just.

It is on his work that civilised society itself depends.

Lord Dennings

Day 10

Back to Supreme Court of India's Court Room No. 1. The time is 10.30 A.M. The scene is much the same as yesterday. The judges are in their seats.

Justice A: You may begin.

Pretty: My Lordships. This is the last day of hearing. I have already given a summary of the development of the law relating to the death penalty in U.K., U.S., Australia, Canada, and India. I have also related the views of the United Nations, Council of Europe and the European Union on the issue. I have also tried to draw your Lordships attention to some leading decisions of this Hon'ble Court on death penalty.

Sometimes issues as the present one, become matter of intense public debate. Everyone concerned wants to join the bandwagon and throw in his or her views - the Press, Lawyers, Politician, Organizations - both for and against the issue. Where does all this lead to? One thing all this does is add to the already existing confusion.

But ever so often, someone does take a purer, unbiased view. Peter Bleach of the Purulia armsdrop case, who was with Dhananjoy Chatterjee at a Kolkata jail before he was released, wrote to the Hindustan Times from Scarborough, UK.

"We were imprisoned in adjacent blocks at the Alipore Central Correctional Home……..He is not a goonda or a mafia boss. He is polite, quiet and poor……He is also illiterate…….

"When I read the trial record, it was obvious Dhananjoy had been convicted on the basis of the most indecisive circumstantial evidence imaginable. There were serious defects in the evidence of certain witnesses. On that basis alone, a conviction, let alone a death sentence, could be safely ruled out.....

"The Supreme Court has specifically directed that when there is undue delay in the execution of a death sentence, that sentence must be commuted to life imprisonment….the prosecutor's primary submission was that the delay in execution was Dhananjoy Chatterjee's own fault! Even more extraordinary, the court accepted that submission…….

"Let's not make any mistake about what is happening here. Dhananjoy is going to be hanged because he is a poor man without any influence. Do we really think he would be hanged if he was a wealthy, upper caste man, a politician, a filmstar or a gang boss with political connections? Of course not. Ways are always found to acquit such people."

DNA Testing

Pretty: My Lordships. Most respectfully, I submit that there is no evidence to convict Ravi Savant. There is no witness. The little evidence on which the prosecution has relied and the trial court has found him guilty is only circumstantial. No DNA testing has been done.

In the case of rape, DNA testing provides conclusive evidence of the guilt or innocence of an accused.

I am reminded of a Florida case. In 1985, Frank Lee Smith was convicted for the rape and murder of 8-year old Shandra Whitehead. He was sentenced to death.

Four years later, in 1989, Chiquita Lowe, a crucial witness for the prosecution, changed her testimony and said that it was Eddie Lee Mosley, not Frank Lee Smith, whom she had seen on the night of the murder. The state Supreme Court ordered the trial judge to hold an evidentiary hearing. This took place in 1991. The judge held Chiquita Lowe's retraction not credible and therefore denied a new trial.

In August 1998, when advanced DNA testing had become available, Frank Lee Smith's lawyers filed an application to get DNA testing done. The judge denied the DNA testing.

In January 2000, Frank Lee Smith died of cancer - in prison - on death row. Finally, pressurized by the defense, the State of Florida, reluctantly allowed his DNA to be tested against what was left in Shandra Whitehead's rape kit. The tests excluded Frank Lee Smith. Eddie Lee Mosley's DNA matched. Frank Lee Smith was exonerated in November 2000 - 10 months after his death.

I would like to tell the Court something about DNA testing. The use of DNA technology in criminal cases began in 1986 when the police asked Dr. Alec J. Jeffreys of Leicester University, England (who coined the term "DNA fingerprints") to verify a suspect's confession that he was responsible for two rape-murders in the English Midlands. Tests proved that the suspect had not committed the crimes. In a 1987 case in England, Robert Melias became the first person to be convicted of a crime (rape) on the basis of DNA evidence.

In one of the first uses of DNA in a criminal case in the United States, in November 1987, the Circuit Court in Orange County, Florida, convicted Tommy Lee Andrews of rape after DNA tests matched his DNA from a blood sample with that of semen traces found in a rape victim.

In a DNA exoneration case, West Virginia paid Glenn Woodall $1 million in an out-of-court settlement. Woodall had wrongfully served four and a half years in jail and another year in home confinement before he was exonerated. This is one of the largest financial awards ever granted. Incidentally, the figure matched West Virginia's maximum insurance coverage carried for such civil suits.

Such damages are not uniformly awarded. In some countries and states, the government is specifically protected from paying damages by sovereign immunity.

DNA testing is expensive but the results have come to be widely accepted. A number of rape convicts the world over have been proved innocent and exonerated on the basis of DNA testing.

Pretty: My Lordships. Most respectfully, I submit that presuming Ravi Savant committed the crimes of rape and murder and is guilty, this is not one of the rare of the rarest cases where a death sentence is called for.

In the three consolidated decisions - Rajendra Prasad and two others, to which I have referred yesterday, by a majority judgement dated 9.02.1979 delivered by Krishna Aiyer, V. R.,this court commuted the death sentence of all the accused.

The facts in State of Uttar Pradesh vs. Devendra Singh were almost identical to this case. That case too involved the unfortunate rape and murder - of a ten year girl. Yet in 2004, this Honorable Court only confirmed the sentence awarded by the Trial Court - imprisonment for life.

Ravi Savant is a young and married person with a wife and children. He is not a habitual criminal. He is not a danger to society. Given a chance, he will most certainly reform. He has already suffered much. I humbly request - Give him that chance.

Pretty: My Lordships. Most respectfully, I submit that presuming again that Ravi Savant is guilty, and even presuming that this indeed is one those rare of the rarest cases, where a death sentence is called for, does not the long delay of more than 10 years in executing him, the pain and suffering he has already undergone, entitle him to commutation of the death sentence at this stage?

In T. N. Vatheeswaran vs. State of Tamil Nadu (1983) 2 SCC 68, the petitioner had been on death row for over eight years. The Supreme Court held that a prolonged delay in the execution of a death sentence is inhuman even if the delay is caused by the accused himself by resorting to various appeals, review petitions, etc. The Supreme Court held that a delay exceeding two years would entitle any person on death row to have his sentence commuted to that of life imprisonment.

In Sher Singh and others vs. State of Punjab (1983) 2 SCC 344, the petitioners had been on death row for a little over five years. They wanted commutation of their sentences on the basis of the decision in Vatheeswaran's case. The Supreme Court held that no hard and fast rule of two years could be laid down. The court thus refused to commute the sentence of death at that stage, but it admitted the petition.

However, in Javed Ahmed Abdul Hamid Pawala vs. State of Maharashtra (1985) 1 SCC 275, the Supreme Court reverted to its decision in the Vatheeswaran case. The petitioner in this case had been on death row for a period of two years and ten months. The Supreme Court again took the view that a delay of over two years would entitle a person to a commutation of the death sentence imposed on him and commuted the sentence of death to life imprisonment on the ground of delay. The decision in this case was delivered by Chinnappa Reddy who delivered the judgment of the court in the Vatheeswaran case also.

The conflict in the above decisions was finally resolved by the Supreme Court in Smt. Triveniben vs. State of Gujarat (1989) 1 SCC 678. A Five-member Constitution Bench overruled the Vatheeswaran case on the point that a two-year delay would entitle the convict to a commutation of sentence into one of life imprisonment. The Court laid down certain rules for calculating the delay.

The Court held that a delay in the disposal of mercy petitions occurring at the instance of the executive would be material. And if there is inordinate delay in execution, the condemned prisoner is entitled to come to the court and request it to examine whether it is just and fair to allow the sentence of death to be executed. My Lordships. There has been undue delay in this case. Ravi Savant's death sentence should be commuted to imprisonment for life on this ground alone.

Pretty: My Lordships. The time has come for a re-look at the death penalty itself.

A century ago, even in advanced countries like U.K., death penalty was imposed for very petty offences. Now the world is moving towards total abolition. In India too, attempts have been made from to time, to restrict or remove death penalty.

In 1931, an abolition bill was introduced in the Legislative Assembly by Gaya Prasad Singh. But a motion for circulation of the bill was defeated after it was opposed by the government. In 1956, a bill was introduced in the Lok Sabha by Mukund Lal Agarwal. This, too, was rejected after government opposition. In 1958, a Resolution for abolition was moved in the Rajya Sabha by the famous actor Prithvi Raj Kapur. He withdrew it after debate. He simply wanted to create a public debate. He felt the purpose had been served.

In 1961, a further Resolution was moved in the Rajya Sabhaby Mrs. Savitry Devi Nigam. This was negatived after debate. In 1962, a Resolution moved in the Lok Sabha by Raghunath Singh received more serious attention. This Resolution was withdrawn, but only after the government gave an undertaking that a transcript of the debate would be forwarded to the Law Commission for consideration in the context of its review of the Penal Code and the Criminal Procedure Code.

The result was a separate Law Commission Report on Capital Punishment was submitted to the government in September, 1967. At pages 354-55, the Law Commission summarized its main conclusions as follows:

"It is difficult to rule out that the validity of or the strength behind, many of the arguments for abolition. Nor does the commission treat lightly the argument based on the irrevocability of the sentence of death, the need for a modern approach, the severity of capital punishment, and the strong feeling shown by certain sections of public opinion in stressing deeper questions of human values.

"Having regard, however, to the conditions in India, to the variety of the social upbringing of its inhabitants, to the disparity in the level of morality and education in the country, to the vastness of its area, to the diversity of its population and to the paramount need for maintaining law and order in the country at the present juncture India cannot risk the experiment of abolition of capital punishment."

There has been a change in the law of capital punishment. The capital punishment should only be awarded in the rare of the rarest cases.

We have already executed far too many innocent people the world over. It is time we reviewed the death penalty. If any proof is needed that mistakes have occurred and innocent persons executed, who can explain better than Chuter Ede, former Home Secretary of Britain.

In the House of Commons, Chuter Ede admitted:"I was the Home Secretary who wrote on Evans' papers. 'The law must take its course.' I never said, in 1948 that a mistake was impossible. I think Evans' case shows, in spite of all that has been done since, that a mistake was possible, and that, in the form in which the verdict was actually given on a particular case, a mistake was made. I hope that no future Home Secretary, which in office or after he has left office, will ever have to feel that although he did his best and no one could accuse him of being either careless or inefficient, he sent a man to the gallows who was not 'guilty as charged'. "

Pretty: My Lordships. The time has come for total abolition even in India. It is time the Supreme Court did what the legislators have failed to do. I repeat the words of Lord Dennings:

"Many of the Judges of England have said that they do not make law. They only interpret it. This is an illusion which they have fostered. But it is a notion which is now being discarded everywhere. Every new decision - on every new situation - is a development of the law.

"Law does not stand still. It moves continually. Once this is recognised, then the task of the Judge is put on a higher plane. He must consciously seek to mould the law so as to serve the needs of the time. He must not be a mere mechanic, a mere working mason, laying brick on brick, without thought to the overall design. He must be an architect - thinking of the structure as a whole, building for society a system of law which is strong, durable and just. It is on his work that civilised society itself depends."

Unfortunately, the decisions have not been consistent and uniform. Why one convict is sentenced to death while another is given the lesser sentence of imprisonment for life remains an insoluble mystery.

Why Judges like Krishna Aiyar and P. N. Bhagbati treat the death penalty as unconstitutional while other Judges treat it as constitutional? Why a Judge like Chinnappa Reddy commutes the death penalty to one of life imprisonment, whereas on almost identical facts and circumstances another judge confirms the death penalty.

My Lordships. In State vs. Cummings 36 Mo.263 278 (1865), Lord Camden, one of the greatest and purest of English judges, said "that the discretion of a judge is the law of tyrants; it is always unknown; it is different in different men; it is casual, and depends upon constitution, temper and passion. In the best it is often times caprice; in the worst, it is every vice, folly and passion to which human nature can be liable."

My Lordships. I have finished. I invite you to declare the death penalty unconstitutional even as the Supreme Court of the U.S. declared the execution of children illegal. And if that be not possible, to commute the death penalty of Ravi Savant.

Solicitor General: My Lordships. Over the last ten days, a lot of cases have been discussed. Ms. Pretty should be complemented on a job well done. Unfortunately, she has a bad case and her client deserves nothing but the death penalty.

Justice A: We reserve our judgement. As a very special case, the Court will sit and announce the decision on the coming Sunday, that is after, two days.

The End

Sunday

The media did not know what to report. Pretty's painstaking work had softened public sentiment. Even those baying for Ravi Savant's blood had mellowed down.

Justice A woke up early. His seven year old grand daughter asked him whether he was going to send Ravi Samant to the gallows. His nine year old grand son ridiculed her. He told his sister that Ravi Savant was innocent and should be let off.

The Court assembled at 10.30 A.M. Justice A complimented Pretty for the hard and sincere work she had put in. He said she had done a wonderful job, even the Advocate General could not have argued better.

Then Justice A announced the Court's decision. The Supreme Court had declined to interfere. In effect, Ravi Savant was to be hanged. The Court decided that he should be Hanged to Death on Monday at 5 A.M.

Pretty could not sleep the whole night. She wept. She did not understand what had happened to the petition she had submitted to the President of India the previous Sunday. She had sat outside the President's House, the whole of Saturday night, just to see him once. Finally, on Sunday, she did obtain an audience. She submitted a petition requesting for a DNA testing. She also requested for Stay of Execution of Ravi Savant till the report came. The

President had assured her that both her requests would be granted. But she should not disclose this to anyone.

The President directed the Central Forensic Laboratory in New Delhi to do the DNA testing. He also directed his office to order stay of execution of Ravi Savant till the DNA reports came, in case the Supreme Court confirmed the death sentence.

The DNA report was expected to come on Monday - the day of execution. The President's office ordered that the execution of Ravi Savant be stayed till further orders. But the communication reached the Jail minutes after Ravi Savant had been hanged.

When Ravi Savant was being taken to the gallows, the Jailor asked him his last wish. Ravi Savant said, "I am innocent. May God forgive all of you." Ravi Savant was hanged on Monday at 5 A.M.

On Monday, the DNA reports came……..Ravi Samant was innocent. But by this time, it was too late. He had already been hanged.

Justice A resigned from his high office. He became a recluse. The President's term was soon over. He returned to his native village a thoroughly disillusioned man. If he had had his say, he would have certainly stopped the death penalty. The Prime Minister and the Home Minister were regretful. But if they had commuted the death penalty, the opposition would have voted the Government out. Ravi Samant's wife disappeared with her children never to be seen again. No one knows whether she moved over to a new place or committed suicide.

The several anti capital punishment organizations added one more name to their list of innocents executed. Ravi Savant passed into the pages of history.

My last thoughts

As I go through the book for the last time before sending it to the press, the unfortunate faces of the innocents who have been wrongly convicted flash through my thoughts; the several families who have been totally devastated. Tears roll down my eyes.

This may be the end of this book. But certainly it is not the end of the fight against capital punishment. The two and a half minutes live video recording of the hanging of Saddam Hussein shown by the media all over the world has rekindled the thinking on capital punishment.

Many readers would not be aware that the Indian Narcotics Drugs and Psychotropic Substances Act prescribes the death sentence for a second conviction under the Act.

On 6 February 2008, a special Narcotics Court in Mumbai sentenced a Kashmiri, Ghulam Mohammed Malik to death, under this provision. The Judge observed that he had no discretion in the matter.

The issue

The issue is not whether a murderer, a traitor, a rapist, or some other person found guilty of a capital crime (where the law permits capital punishment) should or should not be punished. Imprisonment for life itself is a very harsh punishment.

The issue is whether even today any civilized country can retain capital punishment in its legal system. Whether a country like India which talks of Hinduism,

Ahimsa and Forgiveness; and advanced countries like Japan and the U.S., can be amongst the last countries to abolish capital punishment.

More than half of all countries have abolished the death penalty in law or practice; Iraq has now rejoined the small number of countries where executions are routine and justice uncertain. More than 90 per cent of all executions take place in China, Saudi Arabia, US and Iran.

The following is a summary of the latest position as at the end of 2007:

No. of countries which retain the death penalty in their laws 62 (the number of countries that actually execute prisoners in any year is much smaller).

No. of countries that have no death penalty in their laws 91 (In 1977, the corresponding number was only 16.)

No. of countries that have abolished the death penalty in law 135 or practice

Total number of persons executed in 2006, in 25 countries 1591

Country wise list of executions:

China 1,010

Iran   177

Pakistan   82

Iraq and Sudan   65 each

USA (in 12 states)   53

91 per cent of all known executions took place in just six countries - China, Iran, Iraq, Sudan, Pakistan and the USA.

(Executions in Iran and Saudi Arabia are still public. Criminals are beheaded with the sword in Saudi Arabia, and hanged from cranes in Iran, where children under the age of 18 are still executed.)

In the U.S. capital punishment is under attack. It will be abolished. It is only a question of time.

The United Nations has already passed a resolution recommending abolition and calling for a moratorium of pending executions.New Jersey introduced abolition in December 2007. The year 2008 started with Uzbekistan adopting abolition. The world is moving towards total abolition.

Barnali Deb Case

I have recently read the news that the Supreme Court of India has commuted the capital punishment awarded to two convicts to life term in the sensational Barnali Deb rape-and-murder case.

Bishnu Prasad Sinha and his accomplice Putul Bora had kidnapped, raped and murdered Barnali Deb, a seven-year-old girl, and thrown her body into a septic tank when she was sleeping at a bus shelter in Guwahati with her family on July 12, 2002.

Barnali Deb and her family were on their way to Dimapur in a bus and had put up at the shelter owned by Net Work Travels. Sinha was the night chowkidar there.

Bishnu Prasad Sinha and Putul Bora were tried for rape and murder of Barnali Deb. A Kamrup court sentenced them to death. The High Court confirmed the death sentence.

A bench of two judges, headed by Justice S.B. Sinha, said the fact that the convicts had felt repentant after the crime had to be taken into account while awarding the sentence. The other judge was Justice Markandey Katju.

The court observed that the involvement of the accused stood proved beyond reasonable doubt but added that ordinarily, death sentences should not be awarded in cases based on circumstantial evidence. Besides, repentance by one of the accused, who even confessed before a magistrate, could not be overlooked.

The apex court, while commuting the death sentence, observed: "The question which remains is to what punishment should be awarded. Ordinarily, this court having regard to the nature of the offence, would not have differed with the opinion of the learned sessions judge as also the high court in this behalf, but it must be borne in mind that the appellants are convicted only on the basis of the circumstantial evidence."

If Dhananjoy Chatterjee's case had been before this bench, he would have been spared.

Hon'ble Justice V.R Krishna Iyer - to you I dedicate this book

I am indebted to Hon'ble Justice V.R Krishna Iyer for his wonderful foreword which beautifully summarises all that I have to say.

My sincere heartfelt thanks to you.
To you, sir, I most humbly dedicate this book.

www.ingramcontent.com/pod-product-compliance
Lightning Source LLC
Chambersburg PA
CBHW071420170526
45165CB00001B/338